The Communards of Paris, 1871

DOCUMENTS OF REVOLUTION
General Editor: Heinz Lubasz

The Communards of Paris, 1871

EDITED BY STEWART EDWARDS

Cornell Paperbacks
CORNELL UNIVERSITY PRESS
Ithaca, New York

FRONTISPIECE *Communards pose on the débris of the Vendôme Column, demolished as a symbolic attack on the 'brute force and false glory' of the hated Second Empire of Napoleon III.*

Documents translated by Jean McNeil

Picture research by Alla Weaver

© 1973 THAMES AND HUDSON LTD, LONDON

First published 1973 by Cornell University Press.

First printing, Cornell Paperbacks, 1973. Second printing 1981.

International Standard Book Number 0-8014-9140-1 Library of Congress Catalog Card Number 72-13387

Contents

Accompanied by a cheering crowd, Paris Deputies leave the Legislative Chamber (where the overthrow of the Second Empire had been declared) to march to the Hôtel de Ville and proclaim the Republic: detail of a contemporary painting by Jacques Guiaud and Jules Didier.

Introduction

The Paris Commune of 1871 was the biggest urban insurrection of the nineteenth century, an anticipation of the revolutions that were to follow. Its own past lay in the revolts of urban workers against the first effects of industrial capitalism in France; the uprising of the Lyon silk-workers in 1831; further revolts in Lyon and Paris in 1834; the insurrection of workers in Paris in June 1848. The term 'Commune', as well as being the word for the smallest unit of local government, also enshrined the most extreme tradition of the first French Revolution, the organization of the popular districts of Paris into a political body rivalling the authority of the central government. It had been this first Paris Commune that had brought Robespierre to power, had given control of the ruling Committee of Public Safety to the Jacobins, and so had inaugurated the most radical phase of the great French Revolution. And even though Robespierre's Committee of Public Safety had in the end crushed the Commune, 1793 – Year II of the Revolution – remained the great tradition of popular government.

That tradition again came to the fore in 1871. It was now invoked in the face of the defeat of the French army by the Prussians, of the collapse of the existing régime – Napoleon III's 'Second Empire'. On 4 September 1870 the French army had suffered a decisive defeat at Sedan, the Emperor had been captured by the Prussians, the Republic proclaimed, and a provisional Government of National Defence formed. This new government made a show of continuing the war, but was more desirous of negotiating a peace. Soon there developed popular protest against the new 'bourgeois' government for the half-hearted way the war was being conducted and against the attempted peace negotiations. In the autumn and winter there were revolts not only in Paris but in Marseille, Toulouse, Saint-Étienne, Narbonne and Le Creusot. Thus to the war between the French government and Prussia was added civil war between the National Government and insurgent elements in the great cities. The greatest of these cities was Paris; and the Paris Commune was the only revolt that was able effectively to defy the government for any length of time.

The seventy-two days from 18 March to 28 May 1871, the length of time Paris was able to hold out against the National Government at Versailles and its army, though too short to carry out any permanent measures of social reform, were long enough to create the myth, the legend, 9 of the Commune as the first great workers' revolt, the break-up of the power of the State, which was to inspire communists, socialists and anarchists alike in the period up to, and even after, the Russian Revolution of 1917. Marx in London closely followed events in Paris, aided by his contacts in the First International, and immediately afterwards produced his pamphlet, *The Civil War in France*, aimed at showing that a workers' revolution would inevitably have to 'smash the State machine', before it could progress any further. This was about as close to anarchism as the mature Marx ever came. Anarchists themselves have always seen in the Commune the justification for their interpretation of social revolution. Kropotkin, another exile in London, though he admitted that the Commune did not develop sufficiently to mark a break with 'the tradition of the State', wrote that 'a new idea was born under the name of the Paris Commune, one destined to become the point of departure of future revolutions'.[1] Within France itself, the Commune became firmly entrenched in the working-class tradition. In 1880, the very year of the general amnesty for those imprisoned as a result of 1871, one of the former members of the council of the Commune, the shoe-maker Alexis-Louis Trinquet, was elected socialist Deputy for the Belleville district in Paris. During the election campaign 25,000 had responded, despite police attacks, to the socialists' appeal for the first demonstration at the 'Wall' of the Père-Lachaise cemetery, sacred as the spot where some of the last fighting had occurred. The Wall became and has remained a place of annual pilgrimage for socialists and communists.

The following selection of documents seeks to illustrate many of the facets of what was an unplanned, unguided, formless revolution. Besides contemporary documents, many of them archival, there are also the accounts of participants and observers who later wrote their memoirs. Each section has its own prefatory explanation, and there are footnotes elucidating references and other matters in the text. The remainder of this Introduction gives a general survey of the origins of the Commune and of its history, as a background to the documents that follow.

Opposite: above, members of the Government of National Defence formed on the overthrow of the Second Empire in September 1870, among them Adolphe Thiers (fourth from the right), soon to be appointed the Republic's Chief Executive. Six months later Thiers and his ministers fled Paris at the start of the Commune, symbolized in Daumier's cartoon, below, by the female figure of the Republic.

[1] *Actes et paroles*, Paris, 1885, pp. 120, 124.

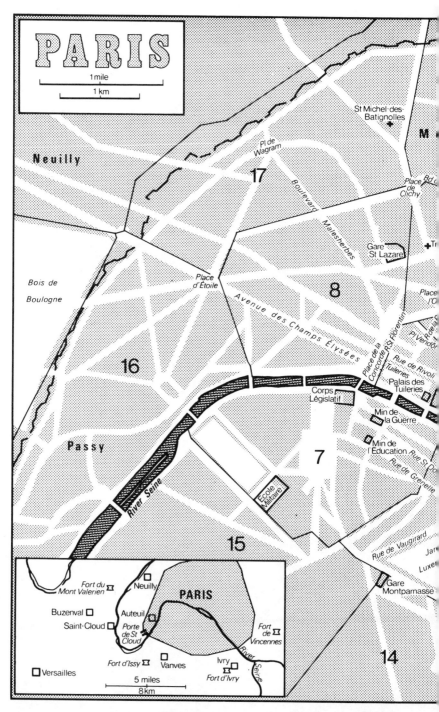

Map of Paris in 1871, showing the boundaries of

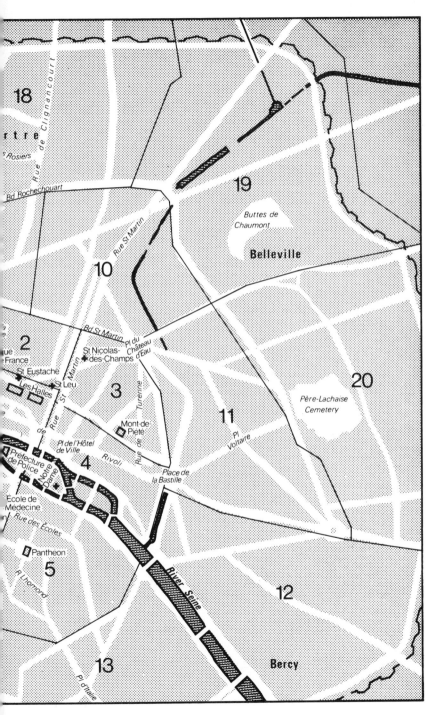

rondissements and the fortified wall encircling the city.

Paris in 1870, on the eve of the outbreak of war with Prussia, was the glittering capital of Napoleon III's Second Empire. Industry supported itself, as it had under monarchies of earlier periods, off the large consumer market the city provided. The luxury trades were able to thrive off the court life re-established in the early 1850s and off the conspicuous spending this encouraged, aided not a little by the influx of rich foreign visitors. But away from the centre where the *beau monde* displayed itself, Paris was sharing in the general industrial development of the north of France. New heavy industries had grown up and had gathered round them a working population, so that eventually in 1860 the city boundaries had to be extended, bringing the number of arrondissements to their present figure of twenty (an arrondissement being a sub-unit of local city government, each one having its own mayor). Many of the new workers in the outer districts were first-generation immigrants from the provinces; others were native Parisians who had been driven from the central districts by the rebuilding schemes of Napoleon and his Prefect of Police, Baron Haussmann. The construction of the new market-place, Les Halles, for example, cut the population of that central district by almost a half in a period of six years. Working people who had formerly lived there were obliged to move further out. Haussmann claimed that he built more accommodation than he destroyed, but the new apartments along the central boulevards were too expensive for most workers, and rent control was rejected as a fallacious socialist theory. It was the by now familiar story of urban redevelopment forcing out the indigenous population.

Thus began the horizontal division of Paris (akin to that of most modern cities) in place of the vertical division that had existed hitherto. Formerly social divisions had formed within the house itself: middle-class people lived on the first and second floors, servants in the basement, or on the upper storeys along with workmen's families and members of *la bohème* – writers, artists and students. Now these divisions tended to become horizontal, to split up not the house but the city: the well-to-do inhabited the inner districts, working men's families and *la bohème* the outer. Yet the links with the old Paris, with central Paris were maintained: many workers kept their former jobs, and their places of work were often in the centre of the city. So were the cafés which artists, writers, students and journalists frequented. And as these links were maintained, so were the revolutionary traditions. Memories of 1830 and 1848 lived on in the consciousness of the *quartiers* of Belleville and Montmartre. There was still the sense of intense life that had marked the old central districts, and this continuing sense of *quartier* explains why the local populations were likely to fight very fiercely for their own areas. Their instinctive response to trouble was the barricade.

14

The industrial development of the outer suburbs was reflected in the higher proportion of industrial workers that were arrested after the Commune compared to June 1848. But the Parisian working population of the end of the Empire was still far from being an industrial proletariat. The 1872 census gave 44 per cent of the working population as industrial, but there were probably only about fifteen factories that employed more than a hundred workers apiece, and a further hundred factories each employing between twenty and fifty workers. For throughout France, Paris included, small-scale production remained the norm. Accordingly sharp distinctions were not made at the time because many small workshops were run by the master-owner with one or two employees occupying just a shop front, where were sold the goods produced at the rear. The most solidly working-class district in all of Paris, and the most revolutionary, Belleville, consisted of Paris-born workers in the traditional crafts rather than in the new factory industries.

THE FRENCH LABOUR MOVEMENT

The labour movement of the 1860s expressed this artisan mentality. It was less hostile to industrial capitalism than to high finance. Its ideal often remained that of the independent owner-producer or, where the size of factories made this impossible, that of production along co-operative lines. The value of labour – labour being understood in an artisanal or agricultural sense – was extolled *vis-à-vis* the corrupting and parasitical nature of finance and trade and the concomitant political jobbery of parliaments. Thus socialism was readily interpreted as meaning that the organization of labour in the form of associations of workshops should come to replace the organization of government. The workers should seek their own salvation. The various 'mutualist' societies asked only to be left in peace to pursue their own affairs. Had not the people made the revolutions of 1830 and 1848, let alone that of 1789, while it was always the bourgeoisie that triumphed? This *ouvriériste* point of view was expressed in the first French edition of the rules of the International Working Men's Association, founded in London in 1864. The French interpreted the declaration that the 'economical emancipation of the working-classes is the great end to which every political movement must be subordinated' as support for their own preference for economic rather than political action. (Marx in London was furious with the French branch of the International for having omitted his qualifying phrase 'as a means', which was not included in the official rules until late in 1871.) Be that as it may, the French labour movement was not left in peace to seek its own emancipation. Strikes occurred, on a growing scale as the decade ended, and troops were used to break them. The officers of the International were arrested, and when new ones were chosen, they were arrested in turn.   15

But the revolutionary traditions were not forgotten by the French working class, and memories of the Paris *journées* were handed down from generation to generation. There was also a left-wing republican tradition of opposition to the Empire. Many Frenchmen had never forgiven Napoleon III for the *coup d'état* by which in 1851 he had overthrown the Republic of 1848. At the extreme wing of the radical movement were the Blanquists, mainly Left Bank students and journalists, who looked to the venerable figure of Auguste Blanqui. His years of imprisonment for revolutionary activity had made the 'old one' into a legend. Blanqui's social and political ideas evolved in the course of a long lifetime, and changed substantially after the failure of the 1848 revolution. But they always retained a commitment to conspiracy which dated back to the days of the secret societies of the 1830s. Blanqui remained convinced that a successful revolution could be made only if there existed a dedicated minority of revolutionists. His revolutionary theory was based on the great 'days' of the first French Revolution, which he understood in terms of the events in Paris itself – the taking of the Bastille, the capture of the Tuileries Palace, the Commune of 1793. Atheism was part of his creed: hence his and his followers' preference for Hébert over what Blanqui called the 'bourgeois metaphysics' of Robespierre. The Blanquists, of whom there may have been some three thousand in Paris by the late 1860s, were organized into cells of ten. They tried to spread their views and to win recruits in all sorts of situations. At demonstrations they would mingle, often armed, with the crowd; they would mix with workers in cafés, or make converts among strikers they met in prison. Some joined the Paris branch of the International, and helped to give it a more revolutionary flavour. They represented, in fact, the only organized revolutionary group in France, a group that was in the forefront of all the radical moves during 1870–71.

PRELUDE TO THE COMMUNE: THE FRANCO-PRUSSIAN WAR

The last two years of the Empire had been marked by a growing movement of political opposition to the existing régime. At the beginning of 1870 Napoleon III was forced to grant greater constitutional liberty. His concessions satisfied neither the Left nor the Right. Radical republicans regarded them as insufficient, and gradually turned public meetings – which were being held to discuss social problems – into veritable revolutionary clubs. (After the Commune one police commissioner said that all the ideas that came to the fore during the Commune had first been aired at these meetings.[1]) The extreme conservatives, on the other hand, regarded the Emperor's concessions as excessive, and were further alarmed by the

---

[1] *Enquête parlementaire sur l'insurrection du 18 mars*, 3 vols., Versailles, 1872, vol. ii, p. 227.

republican opposition movement. This movement could surely have been contained; but the Right at court wanted the prestige of the Emperor heightened as a means of quelling the champions of a Republic. The best means, in their eyes, for raising the prestige of the Empire was to revivify the international prestige of France. When, therefore, in the summer of 1870, Bismarck openly challenged French prestige by proposing a Hohenzollern as a candidate for the Spanish throne – a throne long held to be virtually within the 'patronage' of France – the Right at court pressed the Emperor to accept the challenge and go to war with Prussia. It was out of defeat in this war that the Commune was to arise.

The first great French disaster in the war with Prussia was the surrender of an entire French army at Sedan and the capture of the Emperor by the Prussians. When news of this event reached Paris on 4 September 1870, the first response of the population was to demand the overthrow of the Empire and the proclamation of a republic. The crowd, which consisted of middle-class people as well as of working men, invaded the National Assembly and followed this up by marching to the Hôtel de Ville – the traditional centre of all Paris's revolutions – from whose balcony the Republic was duly proclaimed. Those of the members of the National Assembly who were Deputies from Paris formed themselves into a provisional government, the Government of National Defence, which was to govern Paris, and the whole of France, until fresh national elections could be held. (In the event, such elections were held in February 1871, after a truce had been made with the Prussians.)

The events of 4 September were a disappointment to the revolutionaries in Paris, who had hoped that the fall of Napoleon III would have led to the formation of a more radical government. But republicanism was a sentiment common to much of bourgeois as well as to working-class Paris. It constituted a strong force of social cohesion, and patriotism an even stronger one. These sentiments were further reinforced by the fact that, from 18 September onwards, Paris was under siege. Accordingly revolutionary journalists and the workers' associations at first pledged their support to the new government because of the local and national crisis. But this patriotic support, at first simply embarrassing in its enthusiasm, soon became a threat to the self-appointed provisional government. For the aim of the government was not to prosecute the war but to conclude a peace as quickly as possible in order that elections for a new National Assembly might be held. Elections seemed vital to the government because they would re-establish order by removing the government from the constant threat of being held captive by the popular forces in Paris. As Jules Favre, the Foreign Minister, afterwards admitted,[1] the Paris Deputies had seized

---

[1] *Les actes du gouvernement de la défense nationale. Enquête parlementaire. Dépositions*, Versailles, 1872–75, vol. i, p. 336.

power in order 'to repel the forces of anarchy and to prevent there being a shameful revolt in Paris'. There was in fact a further revolt at the end of October, when the news of the surrender of the second of France's armies, that of Marshal Bazaine at Metz, led to a demonstration similar to that which had earlier overthrown the Empire in September. Several members of the government were actually held prisoner for a time in the Hôtel de Ville. The government therefore had to pursue its peace policy in secret, while it tried to placate by talk, but only by talk, the widespread demand, strongest in the most solidly working-class districts, that neither the capital nor an 'inch' of national territory ever be surrendered. The effect of this popular patriotism was to prolong the siege until the end of January, when as a result of a particularly severe winter, with fuel short and food about to run out, the government finally felt able to announce to the population that a truce had been arranged. Many Parisians still thought this was simply to build up stocks to continue the war, and refused to believe – until it was no longer possible to do so – that the war was finally over and peace decided upon. An armistice was announced on 28 January 1871.

This sense of frustrated patriotism is vital to any explanation of the general hostility felt in Paris towards the National Government. It was 'the elementary, universal and powerful feeling' that had to 'be offended and violated in order for the masses to think of revolt', as one Trotskyist historian of the Commune has rightly emphasized.[1] In its immediate origins the Commune was a patriotic revolt by Paris against a National Government which had made what many regarded as a dishonourable peace. The duplicity of the Government of National Defence in professing war while pursuing peace had thrown off the mask of government; its authority had gone while its power was none too strong. The composition of the new National Assembly, elected on 8 February, gravely aggravated the situation. The monarchist majority of the Assembly, elected by rural France against the republican aspirations of the big cities, only further alienated the capital with open talk of restoring the monarchy and of removing the seat of government from Paris for good. By March 1871 there was widespread resentment against the National Government from within the capital, which after all had borne the hardships of the war almost alone. If the Parisian bourgeoisie was not itself ready for open revolt, its hostility to the National Government, now at Versailles, was so great that it could easily come to sympathize with one, as the early days of the Commune were to show.

In the predominantly working-class districts the siege had had a more concrete effect than simply that of inflaming opinion against the government. The patriotic desire for victory had led to the formation of popular

---

18   [1] C. Talès, *La Commune de 1871*, Paris, 1921, p. 21.

The Executioner, *a cartoon by Pilotell, reflects contemporary opposition to the peace treaty negotiated by Thiers with Prussia. Thiers, assisted by Favre, amputates Alsace-Lorraine from the body of a despairing France, whose only hope lies with the dawning 'Social Republic'.*

clubs, which at first had simply intended to aid the government in its war effort. These clubs had soon turned into centres of political disaffection. The Paris section of the International had been responsible for starting up a number of such clubs, or committees, on the Left Bank and in the central arrondissements on the Right Bank. In the solidly working-class suburbs to the north-east on the Right Bank, however, especially in the 19th and 20th arrondissements, a leading role had been played by Blanquist revolutionaries not affiliated with the International. These clubs or committees were a more or less spontaneous phenomenon, one that sprang up in response to the needs of national defence as seen at a local level, though the public meetings and political agitation of the last two years of the Empire had prepared the way for the formation of such political bodies. These 'republican' or 'vigilance committees', as they were called, had elected their own Central Committee, representing the twenty arrondissements of Paris, which had tried to pressure the government into taking more active measures, both to establish the Republic on a more democratic foundation and in pursuit of the war. The Central Committee of the Twenty Arrondissements had demanded elections for a municipal council, 19 that the Prefecture of Police be abolished, that judgeships be made elective, and that all restrictions on the press and on the right to hold meetings and form associations be removed.[1] That is how the popular forces had understood the idea of a democratic republic. The Government of National Defence had wanted to avoid such concessions. It would not even permit the holding of municipal elections in Paris, for this would have created a threat to its own power by in effect granting Paris its Commune. The issue of municipal elections had been constantly raised by the popular clubs and committees during the siege, and the refusal of the government to give in had driven the popular forces into ever more open opposition.

By the beginning of 1871 the popular forces had formed themselves into a Delegation of the Twenty Arrondissements, whose express aim was to oust the Government of National Defence and install a Commune. The more extreme revolutionaries wanted to take the Hôtel de Ville by force, but a majority of the delegates preferred to hope for a mass uprising to bring about the Commune, and a poster was drawn up in appeal to the Paris population at large. On 6 January 1871, the morning after the first shells of the Prussian bombardment had fallen on the Left Bank, Paris awoke to read the famous *Affiche rouge*: 'The policy, strategy, administration of the Government of 4 September, all alike continuations of the Empire, are condemned. Make way for the people! Make way for the Commune!'[2] At the foot of this poster there were 140 signatures of members of the local vigilance committees and clubs, the majority of them unknown workers who had not previously played any public role. Thirty of the signatories were later to become members of the Commune. But the hoped-for mass uprising did not occur and the extremist revolutionaries decided to stage their own revolutionary *coup*. This merely gave the government a chance to show its strength by firing on the demonstrators before the Hôtel de Ville, the only occasion during the siege when blood was shed among Frenchmen.

For the election campaign in late January and early February the vigilance committees now joined forces with the Trade Union Federation and the International to form what was called the 'Revolutionary Socialist party'. Its candidates gained some 50,000 votes in an all-male electorate of 329,000. The programme of this 'Revolutionary Socialist party' was the organizational and ideological culmination of the vigilance committees and clubs that had developed during the siege,[3] but their support was limited within the city and was never strong enough on its own seriously to threaten the government. It was not this party that frightened the

---

[1] See Documents 1 and 2, pp. 44–47.
[2] See Document 3, pp. 48–49.
[3] See Document 6, pp. 53–54.

government and the bourgeoisie. What really alarmed them was the 'revolution armed' (Marx) in the form of the Paris National Guard, which was soon to carry out revolution in Paris.

This body had its origins in the days after the fall of the Bastille in July 1789. It sprang up as a citizen militia of the bourgeoisie, committed to defending their rights against the despotism of the State and against the passions of the mob. After the Restoration the National Guard declined in numbers and in importance. It became a quasi-honorific institution which many middle-class people of modest means sought to join because membership of it conferred a measure of social as well as civic status. In this way it remained solidly bourgeois. No poor man could join it in any case, because a guardsman had to buy his own uniform, and the uniform was expensive. On the eve of the revolution of 1848 the National Guard numbered no more than about 56,000 men. But with the outbreak of revolution in February 1848 it was suddenly vastly expanded. Its membership grew to about 250,000, and a number of popular battalions were formed, distinguished from the more 'respectable' ones by the fact, among others, that they received uniforms free of charge. The inclusion of so many poor people meant that the National Guard was no longer reliable as a force on the side of law and order: the workers' revolt of June 1848 had to be suppressed by the army. Hence Napoleon III, after he had seized power in 1851, allowed the National Guard to decline in numbers and in importance. Once more it became solidly bourgeois.

In 1870, however, with the departure of the army to the front to fight the Prussian troops, the government could not avoid calling up the sixty bourgeois battalions of the National Guard to defend the fortifications surrounding Paris. The war fever that now gripped the city generated a patriotic demand that *all* citizens be armed. Within a few weeks there were over 130 new battalions, making a total of some 300,000 Parisians in the National Guard. 'No one could call himself a citizen', it was being said, 'unless he had a rifle.' The cry was for more arms, and the authorities were forced to distribute hundreds of thousands of weapons to those flocking to join the newly formed battalions. A few of the new battalions were skilful enough to obtain *chassepots*, the best army rifles, but flintlocks were probably no rarer. Soon the distinction was being drawn between the 'good battalions' – the original sixty drawn from the ranks of the bourgeoisie – and the 'bad', the new battalions into which the lower classes had been enrolled. Often, however, even within the same battalion there were 'good' and 'bad' elements, and the authorities found it increasingly difficult to know which battalions, if any, they could rely on. Yet this was the only armed force within the city throughout the siege: the police, who were unpopular because of their association with the despised régime of Napoleon III, had had to go into hiding.

The National Guard did very little during the siege. Sentry duty had hardly been demanding, since the Prussians had been content to starve Paris out instead of trying to take it by assault. So the men had sat round in cafés or guard posts, complaining of the government's conduct of the war and its refusal to use the National Guard in a mass assault – a *sortie torrentielle* – upon the enemy. The only time the National Guard was used, mainly to placate popular opinion as a prelude to a truce, was on 19 January 1871, at Buzenval. Even then, either out of fear or military prudence (and class prejudice), only the bourgeois battalions were allowed to see any action. There was in any case a long-standing animosity between the army and the Paris populace dating back to the military repression of the workers' uprising of June 1848 and the *coup d'état* of Napoleon III. Under the Second Empire the army had moved away from the republican traditions of the French Revolution towards becoming the defender of a catholic, conservative concept of order, recruiting its officers from among the upper ranks of the bourgeoisie. As for the ordinary soldiers, they were mainly peasants from the provinces, some barely speaking standard French and without sympathy for the constant discussion, pamphleteering and café bravado of the *à outrance*, as the Parisians were called. Had the Government of National Defence seriously wanted to defeat the Prussian invader it would have had to engage in a partisan war across the whole of France. But such a war would have implied a spirit of resistance that on the whole, apart from the big cities, was lacking. It would also have meant, as was so evident in the case of Paris, the revolutionizing of the war. The victories of the famous volunteer battalions of 1792–93 had been won by a revolutionary government, culminating in the ascendancy of Robespierre and the Committee of Public Safety. New tactics and new commanders had been found to replace the generals and parade-ground formations of the *ancien régime*. It was precisely such a social upheaval that the government in Paris wished to avoid. As one of its generals said afterwards, 'the diplomacy of the government and almost all of the defence revolved around one thing: *the fear of a revolt*'.[1]

The conclusion of the war therefore left the National Guard feeling it had been betrayed. During the February election campaign for the National Assembly the National Guard battalions formed their own electoral committees which supported an extreme republican state. After the electoral results showed a marked swing to the monarchist Right throughout provincial France, the Paris National Guard held a further series of meetings, in the latter part of February and in early March, to choose its own Central Committee.[2] The National Government now in effect lost control over the only armed body in the capital, the army having been disarmed

[1] General Ducrot, *La Défense de Paris (1870–1871)*, Paris, 1877, vol. i, p. 215.
[2] See Documents 4 and 5, pp. 50–53.

in accordance with the terms of the truce. The Central Committee of the National Guard lacked any clear revolutionary ideology or organization such as the Committee (or Delegation) of the Twenty Arrondissements had developed. Most of the members of the National Guard Central Committee were ordinary working-class Parisians who had had no previous political experience, though nineteen of them later sat on the Commune. Its mentality was defensive, a patriotic and republican reaction against a National Government felt to be hostile to the wishes and interest of Paris.[1]

Apart from politically radicalizing Paris, the four-month-long siege had left the capital in a state of economic collapse. The winter had been the severest in living memory. Food and fuel had been the main problems, and there were food riots in February as soon as traders brought out stocks they had kept hidden in order to profiteer. Unemployment was widespread. Thousands of demobilized soldiers wandered loose in Paris and joined in the general hunt for food, shelter and warmth. For most working men the only source of income was the 1·50 francs daily pay of the National Guard, which in effect had become a form of unemployment pay. The National Assembly showed no comprehension of the economic realities of the near-starving capital. One of its first acts was to abolish the National Guard pay, the allowance now being obtainable only on proof of need. Thus what had come to be regarded as a patriotic due became something to be begged for. Landlords were allowed to demand the immediate payment of all back-rent owing from the beginning of the siege, which affected all classes except the most wealthy. The petty-bourgeoisie, the numerous small shopowners, were particularly hard hit by a decree making all overdue bills (the *échéances* or promissory notes) repayable with interest during the next four months. As a police chief afterwards remarked, the effect of this latter measure in particular was that, 'though the small manufacturers did not throw themselves into the revolutionary movement, at least they said to themselves that it was not worth while defending the government'.[2]

By March, Paris was in a state of economic and political crisis, which the National Assembly seemed neither able nor willing to alleviate. 'We provincials were unable to come to an understanding with the Parisians', admitted one of the monarchist secretaries of the Assembly; 'it seemed as though we did not even speak the same language, and that they were prey to a kind of sickness.'[3] At the head of the National Government was Adolphe Thiers. He was an astute, hard, unscrupulous, shrivelled-up old man, sure of his own superiority over everyone else around him, with no love for the populace out of which he had long ago assiduously raised himself. As a minister under Louis-Philippe he had seen to the savage

---

[1] See Document 7, p. 55.
[2] *Enquête parlementaire*, vol. ii, pp. 120–21.
[3] Vicomte de Meaux, *Souvenirs politiques*, Paris, 1905, p. 46.

repression of the workers' revolts in Paris and Lyon, of the 'vile multitude' as Thiers was later to call them in a phrase not forgotten in the popular imagination. It was Thiers who, at the time of the 1840 crisis between England and France, had first proposed that Paris be fortified by building a wall round the city covered by forts, and had rebutted his republican critics' charges that he was preparing the means to put down revolts by assurances that no French government would ever think of maintaining itself by bombarding the capital. By the time he took power as the Chief Executive of the Republic he was prepared to abandon his monarchist past in favour of a conservative republic, especially if he could be its head. But he was extremely unpopular in Paris, where the violence of the caricatures knew no limits. He had come near the bottom of the list of Deputies elected by the capital, in marked contrast to his success in the provinces, where he had come top of the list in twenty-six départements.

The details of a peace with Prussia having been quickly concluded (Thiers had already acted as negotiator during the war), he had to face the difficulty of regaining control over Paris. The crux of the problem was how to disarm the National Guard. Thiers had only twelve thousand troops left after the truce to do this with, against several hundred thousand National Guards. He had, moreover, no time, even if he had had the patience, to enter into long-drawn-out negotiations. The rural majority in the Assembly was moving from Bordeaux, where it had held its first meetings to be clear of the Prussians, to Versailles, close to Paris.

The Prussians were still occupying northern France, as security for the payment of the war indemnity which France had agreed to pay as a condition of peace. In order to be able to pay the first instalments on this indemnity, and so to secure the evacuation of northern France by the Prussian troops, the French government would need to raise loans. Money could be raised, however, only if the public had confidence in the new government. Thiers's principal problem was, therefore, the restoration of confidence. Order would have to be re-established, shops opened up, business resumed and life returned to normal. Above all, since Paris was the heart of the nation, Paris would have to be brought under the control of the National Government.

But Paris was defiant. It was not ready to accept a Prussian victory, and that meant that it was not pleased with the government that had capitulated to the Prussians, or with its head, Thiers. Patriotic resentment of French capitulation inevitably meant resentment of the new government at Versailles. The Paris National Guard remained on the alert, ready to resist any forcible entry of the Prussians into Paris. Cannons left over from the siege of Paris were taken to various parts of Paris. In the end, it was only those cannons taken to working-class districts – to the heights of Mont-
24 martre and to the Buttes-Chaumont area of Belleville – that became the

On 1 March 1871 the triumphant Prussian army paraded through a deserted and defiant Paris; black flags hung from the windows, the shops were closed, the fountains stilled. Parisian resentment of the peace treaty was a major factor leading to the 18 March uprising.

critical issue. As Thiers said afterwards: 'businessmen were going around repeating constantly that financial operations would never be started up again until all those wretches were finished off and their cannons taken away. An end had to be put to all that, and then one could get back to business.'[1] Thiers was scarcely an impartial witness, even when he claimed to be quoting. At any rate, he decided to seize the cannons.

THE START OF THE COMMUNE

The government's attempt to capture the National Guard's guns early on the morning of Saturday, 18 March 1871, sparked off the revolution. The plan was to occupy strategic points throughout the city, capture the guns, and arrest known revolutionaries. Thiers himself and some of his ministers went to Paris to supervise the operation. At first, Paris being asleep, all went well. But soon crowds began to collect, jeering at the soldiers, the women particularly remonstrating with the hungry soldiers even while offering them food. The National Guard began to turn out, though surely not in support of the government. The regular troops, still waiting for transport to arrive to cart away the guns, began to find themselves isolated. Events first took a serious turn at Montmartre, when the troops refused to fire on the crowd and instead arrested their own commander, who was later shot.[2] Elsewhere throughout the city officers found they could no longer rely on their men, and in the early afternoon Thiers decided to abandon the capital. Jumping into a waiting coach he scribbled an order for the complete evacuation of the army to Versailles, and summoned the rest of his ministers to follow him.

---

[1] *Enquête parlementaire*, vol. ii, p. 11.
[2] See Documents 8 and 9, pp. 56–65.

By 11.00 that night the Central Committee of the National Guard finally mustered up enough members and enough courage to take over the abandoned Hôtel de Ville, while other National Guard commanders and men occupied the remaining public buildings in the capital. This revolution was a spontaneous uprising throughout the city, there having been no central direction by any of the various National Guard committees. So unlikely was Thiers's plan to succeed, and so ineptly was it carried out, that it could easily seem as if he had deliberately sought to provoke insurrection. Afterwards Thiers set his actions in a historical framework by referring back to his suggestion at the time of the February 1848 revolution that the King should withdraw from Paris. He could also point to the example of the Austrian General Windischgrätz, who by such a tactic had crushed the 1848 Vienna revolution. It may be that Thiers had such thoughts at the time; but he certainly had made no plans for a retreat, and in the scramble to get out of Paris several regiments were left behind. Once at Versailles the Chief Executive regained his composure and set to work to build up a new army, with the connivance of the Prussians, so as to be able effectively to reduce Paris.

The insurgents found Paris open for the taking, but the main concern of the National Guard Central Committee was to 'legalize' its situation by divesting itself of the power that had so unexpectedly fallen into its hands. Instead, therefore, of following up the rout of the army by marching on Versailles, as the Blanquists urged – a plan which might well have succeeded, considering that many soldiers were only too ready to fraternize with the Parisian populace – the Committee entered into negotiations with the only constitutional body left in the city, the Mayors of the arrondissements, to arrange the holding of elections. The Mayors, who were republicans but not revolutionaries, at first refused to countenance such an irregular situation, and the Central Committee wasted a week before it was able to force the Mayors to give the elections for the Commune some sort of official sanction. This search for a return to legality well brings out the moderation of the revolution thus far. The dedicated revolutionaries had more radical plans of action, but the majority within the National Guard was still seeking to work within the established order, not fully realizing that they had gained power and that it was up to them to act as a sovereign body, instead of being limited by a sense of legality as defined by their enemies. As Élie Reclus, the brother of the geographer Élisée, both ardent Communards, asked on voting day: 'What does legality mean at a time of revolution?'[1]

Some 227,000 votes were cast on Sunday, 26 March, when Paris voted the Commune in, voted in fact for the members of a government of its own. This was only half the number inscribed on the electoral registers, but

[1] *La Commune au jour le jour*, Paris, 1908, p. 39.

these dated back to before the war, since when, both before and after the siege, there had been a big reduction in the population. This exodus worked to the advantage of the popular quarters, since it had been mainly the wealthier sections of the population that had left. So too did the proportional system of representation adopted by the Central Committee, which gave more representation to the densely populated working-class districts than had the previous system. The results showed an overwhelming swing to the Left, only about fifteen to twenty moderate republicans being elected, and they soon resigned. The most solidly working-class arrondissements were the most strongly pro-Communard. The list of the Vigilance Committees, which had attracted only a small proportion of the voters in the national elections a month ago, now found itself in the majority. This was not because of a sudden rush of converts to the 'revolutionary socialist' position, but because the republican majority in Paris was now willing to vote for the Commune as a defensive vote against Thiers and the monarchist National Assembly at Versailles. In the working-class districts the victory of the socialist candidates had a more precise meaning; something, it was hoped, would now seriously be done to favour those previously excluded from government.

The Commune was formally installed in the Hôtel de Ville two days later in the glorious spring sunshine of Tuesday, 28 March.[1] The National Guard battalions assembled, the names of the newly elected members were read out, as, wearing red sashes, they lined up on the steps of the Hôtel de Ville under a canopy surmounted by a bust of the Republic draped in red. On high the red flag was still flying as it had done ever since 18 March. Guns saluted the proclamation of Paris's Commune. 'It was a festival of dazzling simplicity', as one observer was moved to describe it.[2]

THE COMPOSITION OF THE COMMUNE

The Commune finally numbered eighty-one members, after by-elections had been held on 16 April to fill some of the vacancies caused by resignations. But sixty was a good attendance. The average age was 38, five members being over 60. Raoul Rigault, the Commune's head of police, was, at 24, the youngest of the fifteen in their twenties, eighteen more having just turned 30. The only foreigner to be admitted, 'considering that the flag of the Commune is that of the Universal Republic', was the Hungarian Léo Frankel, who had met Marx in London, joined the International, and was one of the most active members of the Commune in the area of social reform.

The members of the Commune lacked political experience. Their debates were often rambling, matters being dropped instead of being

[1] See Document 13, pp. 74–75.
[2] E. Lepelletier, *Histoire de la Commune de 1871*, Paris, 1901–13, vol. ii, p. 462.

pushed to a decision, and entirely unrelated points were raised and then pursued. There was considerable personal acrimony, and eventually this led to an open split.[1] The Commune as a whole lacked political leadership. This was especially serious because it had to win a civil war in order to survive at all. It was on questions such as education or the reform of working conditions that, because of the trade-union experience of some of its members, the Commune showed to best effect. Blanqui might just have provided some political cohesion, but he had been picked up by the police in the south-west and spent the second revolution of his lifetime in a prison cell. Charles Delescluze was the most notable political figure from the past to sit on the Commune. He had been a radical Jacobin figure in the 1848 revolution until forced into exile, and was imprisoned when he tried to return secretly. But years on Devil's Island had ruined his health. He could only speak in a croaking voice, and stayed above the personal struggles and quarrels of the Commune until called upon to play a dignified but doomed role at the end, walking deliberately to his death on a barricade at what is today the Place de la République.

About eighteen members of the Commune came from middle-class backgrounds, from which they had extricated themselves during their school and student days. Among these figures were such as Raoul Rigault, the police chief; Jules Vallès, son of a school-teacher, a journalist who edited one of the best papers of the Commune, *Le Cri du Peuple*; Gustave Tridon, son of a rich Burgundian landowner, who had become a Blanquist historian of the Hébertistes of the first Revolution. In all some thirty members of the Commune can be classed as from the professions, or as belonging to *la bohème*, a term of abuse at the time, half of them having been journalists on republican papers. The rest included three doctors, only three lawyers (in marked contrast to the Revolution of 1789), three teachers, one veterinary surgeon, one architect and eleven who had been in commerce or worked as clerks, including the cautious Francis Jourde who was made responsible for the finances of the Commune.

About thirty-five members of the Commune were manual workers or had been such before becoming involved in revolutionary politics. These were mainly craftsmen in the small workshops that made up the long-established trades of the capital. Typical of this group were copper-, bronze- and other metal-workers, carpenters, masons, house-decorators and bookbinders. What is striking is how small a number came from the new heavy industries that had grown up on the outskirts of Paris. Jean-Baptiste Chardon had worked in the railway workshops at Ivry before he was dismissed for absenting himself to speak at public meetings. Émile Duval, a Blanquist who had been very active on 18 March, was an iron-worker and had been a militant in the strikes of 1864 and 1870. But he was shot

[1] See Document 19, pp. 86–91.

Léo Frankel

Édouard Vaillant

Raoul Rigault

Charles Delescluze

Théophile Ferré

Félix Pyat

Though drawn from a variety of political traditions, these leading members of the Commune were united in the defence of Paris and the Social Republic.

when taken prisoner at the beginning of the civil war. Augustin Avrial had been one of the founders in 1869 of the Paris Engineers' Trade Union. But on the whole workers in the new large-scale industries in the factories in the suburbs of Paris had not yet formed their own ways of organization and combat. They had not taken to the International, which strongly reflected the 'mutualist' ideas of the co-operative movement. Workers from the big engineering factory at Cail, for example, had begun to take part in the vigilance committee movement and the National Guard federation during the siege. But when it came to the Commune it seems as if such local leadership as had developed felt too unsure of itself, too unsuited, to play a more important role on a wider scale. This they left to militants from other, more petty-bourgeois, districts.

About forty members of the Commune had been involved in the French labour movement and most of them had joined the International. Their experience in trade unions and workers' associations had made many of them suspicious of political power and this gave their thinking an anarchist tinge more in the tradition of the French socialist-anarchist Pierre-Joseph Proudhon than of the Russian exile Mikhail Bakunin (who did have some followers, however, in Lyon and Marseille). But to label this group Proudhonist implies too definite an ideology for a loose though deep sense that this time the working class should make its own revolution and not let the bourgeoisie reap all the rewards, as it had done in the past. The Commune cannot be sharply divided up into political groupings, let alone parties. Proudhonists, Blanquists, Jacobins, socialists, remain very loose descriptions, and even so do not cover all members. The nineteen members of the Commune who had previously sat on the National Guard Central Committee, as a case in point, had had, with only a few exceptions, no previous political experience. About a dozen members of the Commune were Blanquists, and they were particularly active in the police departments, headed by the Blanquists Rigault and Ferré. Their main hope was to save the revolution by getting Blanqui released, either by effecting his escape from prison or by getting Thiers to agree to exchange him for the hostages held by the Commune – the most notable of whom was the Archbishop of Paris. But Thiers decided Blanqui was far too valuable a captive, and the Archbishop had to go to his death along with about seventy others during the last week of the civil war. 'Jacobinism' covers simply the older members (though they had some youthful followers), who shared a common admiration for Robespierre and who had been involved to some degree in the 1848 revolution. Of these veterans Charles Delescluze was the most notable, the journalist Félix Pyat (a windbag of a conspirator whose white locks commanded far too much reverence on the Commune) the most notorious, and the younger Paschal Grousset, the Commune's Foreign Affairs delegate, the most fiery.

THE POLITICS OF THE COMMUNE

'Time', as Marx said, 'was not allowed to the Commune.' It was almost immediately faced by the problem of war, Thiers's troops beginning their attack on 2 April. The only historical example the Commune could look to was the first French Revolution, particularly the years 1792–93, the time of the Jacobin Terror as a response to foreign invasion. The Commune at first met in secret, on the grounds that it was 'a council of war', but secrecy was not what was expected of a revolutionary assembly. The Central Committee of the Twenty Arrondissements, the International and some of the popular clubs all pressed the Commune to make its sessions public. 30 The Commune did agree to the publication of a summary of its debates in the daily *Journal Officiel*, and in principle agreed to admit the public to its debates. But it proved difficult to find a large enough room, and the problem was never solved. Such theory as was ever formulated in 1871 was based on the ideas of 1793 of popular sovereignty: those elected to represent the people were to act as delegates, not as parliamentary members. The popular clubs in particular several times claimed that sovereignty lay as much with them as with the Commune at the Hôtel de Ville.[1] Those elected by the people were subject to recall by the people, and it was the duty of those elected to report back and remain in constant touch with the sources of popular sovereignty. There was talk in some of the clubs of bringing pressure to bear on the Commune, and attempts were made towards grouping the forces of the clubs so as to be able the better to do this. One club, on 21 May, even proclaimed 'the downfall of the Commune, which is not sufficiently revolutionary',[2] and issued a call to march on the Hôtel de Ville.

Some members of the Commune did try to keep in close touch with the forces that had brought them to power, frequenting the meetings of the clubs in their districts. As one member admitted to a public meeting, 'when Robespierre or Saint-Just arrived at the Convention, they were fortified because they came from the Jacobin or Cordelier club, just as the strength of Marat came because he wrote of what he had heard in the midst of the labouring population'.[3] But in general the members of the Commune became consumed by their own debates and by those of the Commissions that they sat on.

The first thought of the Commune had been simply to appoint delegates to take over the various ministries evacuated by Versailles. These were divided up into eight Commissions, though as a portent of socialist intentions a new department was created, the Commission of Labour and Exchange. These nine Commissions were to be supervised and co-ordinated by an Executive Commission of seven, which at first consisted of the three 'generals' the Commune appointed (the two Blanquists, Émile Eudes and Émile Duval, and Jules Bergeret), who led the Commune's troops in its first *sortie* on 3 April, plus four civilian members. But neither the 'generals', nor the Commune's Delegate at the Ministry of War (of whom there were three during the two months of the Commune, Gustave Cluseret, Louis-Nathaniel Rossel and Charles Delescluze), nor the Executive Commission, were ever able to exert much organizational control over the most vital of all its problems, that of the conduct of its own defence. The only army the Commune had was that which had brought it to power, the Paris

---

[1] See Documents 24–26, pp. 96–99.

[2] P. Fontoulieu, *Les Églises de Paris sous la Commune*, Paris, 1873, p. 208.

[3] G. Bourgin and G. Henriot (edd.), *Procès-Verbaux de la Commune de 1871*, Paris, 1924 and 1945, vol. ii, pp. 457–58.

National Guard. The whole revolution of 18 March had been over the problem of control of the National Guard, and its Central Committee soon made it clear to the Commune that the National Guard was going to maintain its own self-government. The National Guard Central Committee, under the leadership of Édouard Moreau, a man of aristocratic pretensions who had come into prominence on the first night of the revolution, claimed that it alone was the military power of Paris, the Commune being only the 'political and administrative power'.[1] The Central Committee made an attempt to produce its own newspaper, and awarded every one of its members a 'commemorative medal' for his part in the revolution of 18 March. Moreau claimed before the Committee that 'the Commune would have taken a different direction if the Central Committee had remained in power'.

The real truth of the matter was that no one body was able to control the National Guard, which maintained its independence at the most local level. Battalions acted of their own accord, refusing in some cases to fight at all or more often simply failing to turn out for duty. There was constant requisitioning, occupation of churches, schools and other public buildings, as well as sometimes of the private houses of wealthy individuals. Often this expressed the revolutionary determination of local commanders to rout out reactionaries and draft-dodgers and seize any hidden arms, and was done with the agreement of the local municipality. But Paschal Grousset, as Delegate for Foreign Affairs, had to apologize profusely when a battalion invaded the Belgian Consulate in the 8th arrondissement in search of some Parisians they thought had entered to escape military service. Guards were likely to arrest anyone they thought suspect, including their own commanders. The artillery battalions were in effect even more completely a law to themselves, having their own arrondissement committees which refused to merge with the main National Guard Central Committee. Rossel, when he took over at the Ministry of War, was particularly furious that he could not get the large number of cannons theoretically available assembled so that they could be used in the defence of the Commune.

The crisis came at the beginning of May, when the Commune was faced by the imminent fall of the key to the Paris defence, the fort at Issy. In an attempt to strengthen central control the Commune on 1 May accepted the proposal, sprung on the assembly by the Jacobin sexagenarian Jules Miot, to create a five-man Committee of Public Safety. This was a strange, anachronistic mixing of contradictory elements from the first Revolution, for it had been the Committee of Public Safety under Robespierre that on behalf of the National Convention had finally crushed the Commune of Paris. There was a bitter quarrel over the name 'Committee of Public Safety', for though all were agreed that the Commune needed a stronger

[1] See Document 15, pp. 79–80.

central power, many felt that the title was no longer relevant to a 'republican socialist movement. What we represent is the period that has passed between '93 and '71. . . . Let us use the terms suggested to us by our own Revolution.'[1] But too many in the Commune had their heads full of slogans of 1793, the civil war making comparisons with that earlier epoch of foreign invasion only too simple. On the whole it was the members closest to the labour movement – a minority – who opposed this 'pastiche of the Revolution', as the future socialist leader Édouard Vaillant called it, the Jacobins and Blanquists – together forming a majority – being generally in favour. Twenty years earlier Marx had written that 'the social revolution of the nineteenth century cannot draw its poetry from the past, but only from the future. . . . In order to arrive at its own content, the revolution of the nineteenth century must let the dead bury their dead.'[2] But many of the Communards slipped only too easily into trying to play the roles of their great ancestors and were not willing to let the dead bury the dead. For the Revolution of 1789 had remained a living force in France and nothing was more natural than that the Commune should seek to interpret itself as a continuation of the revolutionary movement, just as it in turn became a historical model for revolution in Europe in the twentieth century.

This division between 'majority' and 'minority' lasted throughout the final three weeks of the Commune, the 'majority' holding separate meetings from which the 'minority' were excluded. The latter published a protest against the formation of the Committee of Public Safety.[3] The clubs and the popular press, however, welcomed the formation of the Committee of Public Safety. They saw it as a 'revolutionary measure', as showing that the Commune was going to exert greater 'energy' to assure the success of the revolution in Paris.[4] But this was a fond hope, with the 'majority' tending increasingly to act as though they were the supreme body, once even talking of arresting the Committee of Public Safety itself. The division within the Commune did nothing to improve the conduct of the war; it only made the chain of command, such as it was, still more confused. Rossel, the ex-army officer who had joined the Commune out of patriotic revulsion against the surrender to the Prussians, took over the Ministry of War on the day the Committee of Public Safety was formed. In the nine days he was there he made a desperate effort to create out of the National Guard a small effective fighting force, supported by artillery and such cavalry as could be mustered, a force capable of taking the offensive and giving Paris at least a respite. The general disorder left little enough hope

---

[1] Gustave Courbet, quoted in Document 20, p. 93.

[2] *The Eighteenth Brumaire of Louis Bonaparte* in Marx-Engels, *Selected Works*, London, 1968, p. 99.

[3] See Document 21, pp. 93–94.

[4] See Documents 22, 23 and 27, pp. 94–95 and 106–7.

for any attempt to bring about the efficient organization of the forces of Paris. Rossel found himself opposed on all sides, by the National Guard Central Committee, by the Committee of Public Safety and by the 'majority' of the Commune. Commanders in the field were by-passing the Commune's Ministry of War and appealing directly to their friends on the Commune, while National Guard commanders complained they no longer knew whose orders to obey. In desperation Rossel challenged the National Guard to get at least twelve thousand men out on the Place de la Concorde, but only just over half turned up on the morning of 9 May. The same day Rossel received the news that the fort at Issy had finally fallen, and he sent off his resignation to the Commune, accusing it of being the greatest obstacle to victory.[1]

Rossel's resignation and the news from Issy plunged the Commune into turmoil, with members accusing each other of being to blame. The National Guard Central Committee suddenly rallied to Rossel, and the editors of the most popular of the Communard papers, Le Père Duchêne, named after Marat's paper of the first Revolution, pressed Rossel to use the Central Committee and its battalions to overthrow the Commune and save the revolution. Rossel was not willing to try for the role of a Bonaparte, and instead went into hiding until his arrest in June. He was court-martialled and shot. Rossel's place at the Ministry of War was taken by Delescluze, and Pyat, whose rancour and rhetoric had done little but harm, was forced to resign from the Committee of Public Safety. But Delescluze had no knowledge of military affairs, and his appointment marked the end of any attempt at a serious military effort by the Commune. All was to be left to the barricades, the traditional form of street fighting which the Paris working population could manage irrespective of any central control.[2]

THE COMMUNE AS A WORKING-CLASS GOVERNMENT

The actual social legislation passed by the Commune seems reformist rather than revolutionary, taking up demands that had been formulated by the labour movement during the preceding twenty to thirty years. Immediate issues that had to be faced were the problem of arrears in rents and of overdue bills (the échéances), which the central government had so ineptly decreed should be at once repaid.[3] Rents owing for the period of the siege were cancelled, but otherwise the rights of private property were not questioned. After much debate a three-year delay was granted for the payment of outstanding bills. Taken together these were measures that shocked bourgeois opinion outside Paris. Flaubert, for example, indignantly

---

[1] See Document 18, pp. 84–85.
[2] See Document 59, pp. 160–61.
34   [3] See Document 14, pp. 78–79.

declared that the Commune was 'interfering in matters of natural law by intervening in contracts between individuals'. But as Marx more soberly saw from London, these were measures 'favourable to the working class, but above all to the middle class'. A similar issue was that of the State Pawnshop, the Mont-de-Piété, where many workmen had pawned their household goods and finally their tools in order to survive the siege. The central government had threatened to start selling off all unredeemed goods, whereas the Commune followed the practice of previous French governments at a time of national disaster and allowed the free restitution of household articles and work tools up to a certain value. More extreme proposals that the institution be abolished in favour of some form of a working men's bank were not followed up.

The Commune's most innovative social reforms were carried out by, first, the Commission of Labour and Exchange, presided over by the Hungarian Léo Frankel, a jeweller, an acquaintance of Marx and a future activist of the socialist movement both in France and Hungary; and second, the Education Commission, headed by Édouard Vaillant, who had been a science student until the outbreak of the war and later was to be a leading parliamentary socialist figure of the Third Republic. Frankel's Commission was concerned with working conditions, which it tried to improve a little by such measures as abolishing the Empire's system of *placeurs* and *livrets de travail* in favour of letting the mairies (town halls of the arrondissements) act as employment exchanges. Most notably Frankel supported the bakers in their demand for the abolition of night-work, which the Commune granted after some debate in face of opposition from the employers.[1] But the most pressing problem was that of unemployment.

At Frankel's insistence the Commune took the radical step of allowing trade unions and workers' co-operatives to take over factories not in use in order to start up manufacture again. It was primarily a measure directed against those employers who had left Paris, and some form of compensation was promised them should they return. On the side of the Commune there was the feeling that 'wealth' should not be left unproductive; that property should not be exempt from some sacrifices at a time when people were out of work and starving. But more extreme suggestions that 'all the big factories of the monopolists' should be taken over by the workers were rejected. During the Commune the main area in which co-operatives could function was military supplies, and Frankel's commission presented a report reminding the Commune that 'the Revolution of 18 March was accomplished solely by the working class. If we do nothing to assist this class, we who believe in social equality, I can see no reason for the Commune's existence.'[2] The report criticized the Commune for continuing the

---

[1] See Document 49, pp. 136–39.
[2] See Document 46, pp. 130–33.

established practice of accepting the lowest tender, thus forcing wages down. Instead the Commune should buy only from workers' co-operatives and at a fair wage. The Commune was more cautious than its Commission, but did agree to include a minimum wage rate in its future contracts and to show a preference for co-operatives.

Clothing for the National Guard was largely women's work, and here Frankel had the outside backing of what was in effect the women's branch of the International, the 'Women's Union for the Defence of Paris and for Aid to the Wounded'. This had been founded in April by Élisabeth Dmitrieff, the daughter of a Russian hussar, who had escaped the confining conditions in Russia by a *mariage blanc* with an officer much older than herself. As a result of a stay in London in 1870 she had met Marx and become friendly with his daughters. She escaped back to Russia after the Commune, married a prisoner condemned to deportation in Siberia, whence she followed him and died. Élisabeth Dmitrieff, with Frankel's support, pressed the Commune to let her union alone clothe the National Guard so as to provide work for the 'feminine element', and thus to engage it on the side of the revolution.[1] Some such co-operatives were started, but they were not given the monopoly they had asked for.

The idea of co-operation went back to the beginning of the labour movement. It had made Louis Blanc's book, *The Organization of Labour*, a socialist best-seller when it came out in 1839. During the 1848 revolution over three hundred meetings had been held with the aim of forming such associations. The idea got a new lease of life at the time of the Commune. The engineers made attempts to reorganize arms production on a co-operative basis. At the Louvre munitions factory the workers even drew up their own statutes and elected a workers' council to run the factory.[2] But this experiment in workers' control did not get very far, and one of its leaders admitted that too much time was spent in talking and that little work was done. But by 14 May forty-three producers' co-operatives had been formed among the many craft industries in the city, though most of these were formed in anticipation of getting work. The 'State catering service', the café waiters, concièrges, shoemakers, tailors and many others made such proposals. Although few of these amounted to much, they are indicative of the strong current within the working class towards co-operative production.

In the field of education the main effort, at a time when about one child in three under the age of sixteen was getting no formal schooling whatever, was to provide a basic elementary education for all. The initiative here too came from the local level, often from the Mayors or from educational reformers, and the Commune and Vaillant's Commission simply had to

---

[1] See Document 48, pp. 135–36.
[2] See Document 44, pp. 127–30.

support them. The reform movement was strongly against the Church schools, which accounted for over half the total number of schools in Paris. National Guards were used to evict the priests and nuns and replace them by republicans. The emphasis was to be on the secular and scientific side, on the provision of what was called a 'professional' education, by teaching a useful trade as well as more general scientific theories and the humanities.[1] This idea, too, went back a long way, and had been debated at the congresses of the International. The aim was to provide an education suitable for the working man, yet one not so narrowly specialized that the separation into educated and uneducated classes would be perpetuated. Lack of education was felt to be one of the gravest handicaps of the working classes compared to their employers, and this deficiency the various schools set up under the Commune were intended to remedy.

Women's education was given special attention, having been the most neglected area. This had been a demand of liberals and socialists for a long time, though one section of the French Internationalists, the Proudhonists, had strongly argued in favour of the traditional view that a woman's place was in the home, bringing up the family. During the Commune, however, a special Commission was formed with an all-female membership to oversee the attempts made to set up girls' schools. Day nurseries, to be situated near the factories, were also proposed as a means to help working women.[2]

None of these schemes – of co-operative industrial organization or of educational reform – could come to much: there was too little time, and there was a war to be won if anything at all was to be retained. Shortly after the fall of the Commune Vaillant said that 'the streets had simply been cleared and the schools filled in order to leave the population free to fight', though he did add that he thought 'the main lines of an egalitarian education had been sufficiently mapped out for the idea to start to spread'.[3]

More important than any particular measure was the very existence of the Commune as a government that included a substantial proportion of working men and one that, for once, seriously intended to improve the lot of the majority of the population. Hence the many appeals from workers in all trades to the Commune for help, for, as Frankel's Commission said in response to the appeal of the 'Women's Union', the 'Commune is not simply the administrative municipal authority, but above all the affirmation of sovereign power . . . *as a means* towards realizing the very aim of the revolution, namely the emancipation of labour'.[4] Hence too Marx's

---

[1] See Documents 34–36, pp. 113–15.

[2] See Documents 37–39, pp. 115–20.

[3] In a letter dated 31 December 1871, reprinted in M. Dommanget, *L'Enseignement, l'enfance et la culture sous la Commune*, Paris, 1964, p. 158.

[4] See Documents 40–46, pp. 123–33.

Manning a cannon directed at Paris, Thiers (then well over seventy) pleads with death to allow him time to crush the Commune: cartoon by Moloch.

CI-GIT
ADOLPHE
THIERS

judgment on the social work of the Commune: 'the great social measure of the Commune was its own working existence. Its special measures could but betoken the tendency of a government of the people by the people.'[1] Federalist interpretations of the Commune as simply a movement for communal, municipal liberties miss this social dynamic of the Commune: the revolt of 18 March became a revolution. Federalism had been a theme of republican, as of monarchist, opposition to the Empire, and French socialists had in general accepted the federalist ideas of Proudhon. It was a Proudhonist who had drafted the Commune's 'Declaration to the French People', published on 19 April, and during the time of the Commune provincials within the besieged capital held a series of meetings of their regional groupings. Outside Paris plans were made for holding a series of regional congresses in some of the major provincial centres. But the government at once forbade these, and would listen to no overtures made on behalf of Paris. Thiers and his ministers at Versailles had no doubt, however much moderates might wish for reconciliation, that the Paris Commune was a declaration of social change that had to be crushed by civil

[1] *The Civil War in France* in Marx-Engels, op. cit., p. 297.

war. This was a view that was shared by governments outside France, for the very existence of the Commune roused the fury of the European bourgeoisie. The British Press labelled the Communards 'communists', and on 29 March *The Times* described the revolution as 'the predominance of the *Proletariat* over the wealthy classes, of the workman over the master, of Labour over Capital'. The Russian Emperor pressed the German government not to hinder the French repression of the Commune, because the government at Versailles was 'a safeguard for both France and all of Europe', and Bismarck threatened to use the German army if Thiers did not hurry up.[1] It is from the Right as much as from the Left that the socialist nature of the Commune can be, and was, seen.

A 'FESTIVAL OF THE OPPRESSED'

In many ways the most striking aspect of the Commune today is not its social reforms, though its attempts at 'workers' control' are still very relevant, but the festive nature of revolutionary Paris. The atmosphere within the capital was not that of a city dominated by war. There seems to have been no sense of imminent danger, although gunfire could be heard all the time, partly because it was hardly thought credible that the troops of Versailles might actually enter Paris. After the defeat many claimed that they had known the cause was hopeless from the start, something that became obvious before very long. But the young Louis Barron, disillusioned after several weeks at the War Ministry, was probably typical in letting himself be carried along by day-to-day events. The fine weather after the winter of the first siege gave people a sense of light-headedness. Stories of the massacres following the June uprising of 1848 were not taken as a warning. It was thought that at worst the leaders of the National Guard or the members of the Commune would be arrested, but that the population as a whole would surely remain unscathed. Activity kept many from thinking about the future. It was too like a game to give rise to sombre thoughts, this war and this city, which had 'all the signs of being simply on holiday'.[2]

The Commune was indeed a 'festival of the oppressed', as Lenin once described it. The first great festival had been its own proclamation;[3] but this carnival spirit was not to last. Soon the mood became grave. The funerals of National Guardsmen killed in the fighting became grand processions across the city, headed by members of the Commune, and anyone who refused to bare his head was forced by the hisses of the crowd

---

[1] G. Bourgin, 'Une Entente Franco-Allemande: Bismarck, Thiers, Jules Favre et la répression de la Commune de Paris' in *International Review of Social History*, vol. i, 1956, pp. 41–53.

[2] See Document 52, pp. 143–44.

[3] See Document 13, pp. 74–75.

to comply. Another moment of drama was provided when the Freemasons rallied to the Commune, and marched with their banners, never seen before in public, to the city walls, where firing stopped and they sent off a deputation to see Thiers. There were other symbolic ceremonies, akin to exorcisms, such as the public burning of a guillotine which had been discovered by a local committee in the 11th arrondissement.[1] The Commune decided to pull down the Expiatory Chapel for Louis XVI erected by Louis XVIII at the time of the Restoration, and decreed that a chapel erected in memory of one of the generals killed in the June 1848 uprising should suffer the same fate. Neither of these destructions actually occurred, but the Commune was successful in its most ambitious enterprise, the demolition of the Vendôme Column. This had been erected to his own glory by Napoleon I, and under the Second Empire of his nephew it had become a symbol of empire hated by all republicans. The ceremony took place on 16 May before a specially invited crowd, with a larger one in the streets around.[2] Afterwards photographs were taken of National Guardsmen, women and children posed around the fallen column. 'The excitement was so intense', an English observer wrote, 'that people moved about as if in a dream.'[3] Even on the very day the Versailles forces broke into Paris – Sunday, 21 May – there were large crowds in the Tuileries Gardens listening to one of a series of concerts given in aid of the wounded, widows and orphans.[4]

The festivity, the gayness of the capital in its revolution and despite the war, was remarked on by several observers; Villiers de l'Isle-Adam was enraptured by a Paris that preserved within its 'formidable walls' places 'where people still laugh'.[5] To this extent the Commune was the reconquest of the city by the greater part of the population, driven out to the suburbs by Haussmann's redevelopment schemes. The centre was taken over once again by the crowds the police had previously kept at bay. For a time, too short to make any lasting conquests, a large part of the population became actively involved in public affairs, either at the level of their district or at that of the whole city. Order, as repressively understood, was restored only when this population was driven off the streets and its barricades destroyed.[6] Once the city was again under its control, the National Government could celebrate its victory by its own monument in 'expiation' of the 'crimes' of the Commune, the Sacré-Cœur, a white basilica built to dominate what had been red Paris. This struggle for control of urban space was also typified during the fires of the last week of the Commune. Many of these

---

[1] See Document 56, p. 150.   [2] See Document 55, pp. 146–48.
[3] Colonel Stanley, quoted in A. Horne, *The Fall of Paris*, London, 1965, p. 351.
[4] See Documents 53 and 54, pp. 144–46.
[5] See Document 50, pp. 140–42.
[6] See Documents 63 and 66, pp. 163–65 and p. 169.

were started by the Communards as a means of defence, but a few, particularly those of the Prefecture of Police and of the Tuileries Palace, were lit deliberately, as acts of revenge on the class that had built such monuments to its own power. To the Communards their street-by-street defence of Paris was comparable to similar stories of heroism by an invaded population: to the resistance of the Spanish against Napoleon I, for example.[1] The rebuilding after the Commune of most of these monuments, particularly the Vendôme Column and the Hôtel de Ville, *in exactly the same style as before*, was meant to efface the Commune from history by removing all visible signs of it from Paris.

THE END OF THE COMMUNE

The end of the Commune lay in its beginning: Paris had either to rally the people of France to its cause, or to succumb, sooner or later, to the National Government and its army. There was, in fact, not even a question of rallying most of the people, for most of the people were peasants, and most of the peasants were anything but revolutionary republicans. What hope there was for the survival of the Paris Commune lay with the other great cities, and even that hope was quickly dashed. Four days after the beginning of the Commune in Paris a Commune was proclaimed at Lyon (22 March): a day later one was proclaimed at Marseille. But the Lyon Commune collapsed almost as soon as it had begun, on 25 March, and the Marseille Commune was defeated ten days later, on 4 April. There were minor uprisings in other cities in the last days of March, but in practice they were of no consequence. Paris alone, heavily fortified as it was and with a substantial military force at its disposal, was able to hold out against Thiers and the army – for two months.

The army's infantry began to move on Paris at the beginning of April; its artillery began to bombard the city on 1 May. The fort of Issy, to the south-west, fell on 9 May, the fort of Vanves, to the south, on 13 May. On 21 May government troops entered Paris. That, however, was not the end. There followed a week of bitter and bloody street fighting, all the more bitter and all the more bloody because the Parisians could no longer hope to win. *La semaine sanglante*, as it came to be called, was not so much the last campaign in a military encounter as the final outburst of a political struggle; it pitted the human substance of the Commune against the substantial presence of the French State. All the pent-up hostility of the Parisian radicals – most of the non-radicals having long since fled, or keeping to their quarters – poured, quite literally, out on to the streets. Barricades and street fighting, the traditional warfare of the urban insurgent, were simply the last resort of the Commune's struggle for revolutionary self-government.

[1] See Document 65, pp. 168–69.

The uniformed government troops assaulting the people's barricades and pursuing men and women down 'their' streets have entrenched themselves in the legend of the Commune as the very image of political oppression. It is the people's barricades and the street fighting, not the earlier forays of the National Guard or the defence of the Paris forts, which have entrenched themselves in the legend of the Commune as the very image of political defiance.

It was the working-class districts that fought to the bitter end. It was the working population that bore the brunt of the repression that followed.

Judging the Commune as a revolution, it was not just a further stage in a gradual social process – in fact it set back the labour movement in France – but a 'tiger leap', one of those moments that jump forwards in history.[1] Like the practice of some of the Communard papers of dating themselves according to the Revolutionary Calendar of 1792 and thereby treating the intervening period as if it had never existed, the Commune in certain of its manifestations sought to break the continuum of history, to cast off the weight of the past that lies so heavy on the living. This is why the Commune can be seen as a success in spite of its immediate failure, though judged in terms of politics as the art of the possible, of the necessary compromise, it was a senseless revolt in impossible circumstances. But as the upsurge of a repressed population against conventional wisdom with its counsel of prudence, as the attempt to develop extensive forms of social freedom, the Commune was a truly revolutionary event, the breakthrough, however fleeting, into a new realm where what seemed barely possible suddenly becomes actual, and so reveals all other forms as condemned. For this reason it provided an inspiration for European socialists and anarchists. Lenin in 1917 counted the days to see whether the Bolsheviks could hold on to power longer than had the Communards.

Opposite. The Commune collapsed only after a week of bitter street fighting behind barricades and fires: the ruins are of the rue Royale, looking towards the Madeleine. Beneath, sentence is pronounced at the trial before the Third Council of War in September 1871. Of those members of the Commune who were captured, only two were shot, the rest being condemned to transportation. Far more indiscriminate was the unregulated slaughter of some 25,000 people in the streets.

[1] The phrase comes from Walter Benjamin's 'Theses on the Philosophy of History' in *Illuminations*, London, 1970, pp. 263–65.

Part One: Prelude to the Commune – The Siege of Paris

This first group of documents shows how in the special enclosed condition of beleaguered Paris, where there was practically a political vacuum after the collapse of the Empire, there developed a political consciousness, expressed in the formation of republican and patriotic political groups that prepared the way for the Commune. The Paris section of the International and the Blanquists were largely responsible for the formation of the Vigilance Committees, which by the end of the siege had become the most revolutionary and socialist bodies in the city. This movement started, as its first proclamation of 15 September shows (Document 1), with a broad republican appeal for the patriotic defence of Paris. To further its demands the Central Committee of the Twenty Arrondissements, with the backing of other similar groups, pressed for the holding of municipal elections, which would have given Paris its own communal authority alongside the self-proclaimed Government of National Defence. When the government refused to grant elections, the republican committees called on the population to carry them out, regardless of the government's prohibition (Document 2). Nothing came of this attempt, though mayoral elections were granted after the uprising of 31 October. Finally, just before the surrender of Paris, this same republican committee movement, giving itself the more revolutionary title of the Delegation of the Twenty Arrondissements, called for an uprising to carry itself to power and establish the Commune (Document 3).

1 Public proclamation

LIBERTY   EQUALITY   FRATERNITY

Republican Central Committee of the Twenty Paris Arrondissements for National Defence

Citizens,

On 5 September, on the very morrow of the proclamation of the Republic, a great many citizens advocated the formation of a *Republican Central Committee* drawn from the twenty Paris arrondissements. Its function would be to protect the Nation and lay down the foundations of a truly republican régime, calling upon the permanent participation of individual initiative and popular solidarity.

Since that day public meetings have elected their own *Defence and Vigilance Committees* in each arrondissement.

As soon as the majority of the arrondissements were represented by four delegates each on the Republican Central Committee, this Committee went into operation.

It submitted to the Government of National Defence a series of proposals to which the public meetings had given their support.

Public Safety

The Police is to be abolished in the form it takes under all monarchist governments, where it serves to oppress and not to defend the people.

It is to be handed over to the control of the elected municipalities.

Magistrates shall be appointed in every neighbourhood of the large towns, with direct and personal responsibility for the maintenance of public safety.

The special corps of the old centralized Police shall be disbanded, such as the Sergents de Ville, the agents of the so-called Sûreté Publique[1] and the Paris Guards.

The National Guard, drawn from the entire voting population, and particularly the veterans from its ranks, shall assist the new magistrates of the Municipal Police in the performance of their functions.

All members of the judiciary shall be subject to the principles of election and responsibility.

All laws of a restrictive, repressive and fiscal nature against freedom of expression, assembly and association shall be repealed.

Supplies and Housing

All food and other essential commodities at present stocked by wholesale or retail merchants in Paris shall be compulsorily purchased for public use. The dealers are to be issued receipts for these goods and guaranteed payment after the war at the original prices.

In every street, or at least in every neighbourhood, a commission shall be elected to draw up an inventory of all commodities and to declare the present holders of these goods personally accountable to the municipal administration.

These supplies are to be classified into various categories and shared out among the population of Paris in exchange for tokens, which will be distributed periodically in each arrondissement on the basis of (1) the size of the citizen's family; (2) the quantity of goods available as established by the above commissions; (3) the expected duration of the siege.

The municipalities must also provide every citizen and his family with adequate living accommodation.

[1] The French C.I.D. or F.B.I.

The Defence of Paris

Immediate elections must be organized for officers of the Garde Mobile[1] since up to now the men have had their leaders imposed on them.

We must rally as quickly as possible the scattered elements of our heroic army. It has been defeated and disbanded through the treachery of its leaders, and has proved incapable of defending the country since it was organized for repression.

All citizens shall be issued as soon as possible with long-range weapons and sufficient cartridges and ammunition so that they will be fully prepared to fend off attacks.

Each of the twenty arrondissement committees shall be responsible for organizing the necessary equipment and manpower for the defence of each neighbourhood.

All vacant premises, such as abandoned apartments and public buildings, are to be appropriated for the use of the various defence services.

All persons who for any reason have not been called up to serve as National Guards shall be employed in defence work.

The people shall have powers of supervision over all defence operations.

All defence positions within the capital shall be brought into use, including all secret passages and other devices that may be used for the destruction of the enemy, even by women and children. Republican Paris has resolved to be buried under its ruins rather than surrender.

Defence of the Départements

The mass mobilization of all Frenchmen without exception and the general requisition of everything that may be used for defence purposes is decreed.

Support shall be given to all organizations born of popular initiative whose aim is to help safeguard the Republic.

National delegates for defence must be appointed, who will join forces with the Republicans of the départements to stimulate the patriotic zeal of the population, combat reactionary manœuvres, resist treachery and lead the march of volunteers to the rescue of Paris, sacrificing their lives if need be.

In proposing these emergency measures the undersigned are convinced that the Government of National Defence will lose no time in implementing them in the form of decrees for the safety of the Nation and the Republic.

First proclamation by the Central Committee of the
Twenty Arrondissements, 15 September 1870: *Les
Murailles Politiques Françaises*, vol. i, pp. 90–1.

---

[1] Of the National Guard.

Appeal for elections

Citizens,

As you all know, several delegations from the Republican Central Committee, the arrondissement committees, the public meetings and finally, on two separate occasions, a large number of National Guard battalion commanders have insistently demanded the immediate election of a Paris Municipal Council.

We have never intended to mount a partisan opposition to the Government of National Defence in the interest of any particular individual, group or class.

Our only aim is to enable the people of Paris, who are fighting for the defence of the Great City, to exercise their indefeasible municipal rights in agreement with the most natural and basic republican principles.

Far from provoking conflicts, the Central Committee merely intends to use its influence and moral power to stimulate the people into assuming, through fairly elected delegates, the management of their present affairs and the responsibility for their future.

Only if it has an elected municipality can our besieged and heroic Capital gain effective control of its finances, arm itself rationally and organize the fair distribution of supplies.

Citizens,

We have every faith in your political intelligence and in your energy. We entreat you to take upon yourselves the task of forming your own Municipal Council.

At your public meetings, in your arrondissement committees, in your National Guard battalions, right now you must select the men most worthy to represent you at the Hôtel de Ville. It is both the right and the duty of the people of Paris to assume the leadership in this supreme effort to deliver Paris from the foreign invader and to protect the Republic from reactionary forces.

To the polls, citizens, so that our principles may triumph, and at the same time, to arms, for we must defeat the enemies of France.

Appeal to the Paris population by the Central Committee
of the Twenty Arrondissements to hold elections:
Le Combat, 5 October 1870.

3 L'Affiche rouge

TO THE PEOPLE OF PARIS

Has the Government that took over the defence of the Nation on 4 September fulfilled its mission? No!

We have 500,000 men in arms and we are encircled by 200,000 Prussians! Who is responsible for this if not those who govern us? Their only thought has been to negotiate instead of casting cannon and manufacturing arms.

They have refused mass mobilization.

They have left the Bonapartists alone and have thrown the Republicans in gaol.

They have finally decided to take action against the Prussians, but only after two months, on the morrow of 31 October.

Their slowness, their indecision, their apathy have led us to the brink of disaster. They have been incapable of governing and of fighting although they had all the resources, supplies and men they needed.

They could not see that in a besieged city all those who participate in the defence effort have an equal right to receive support from the Nation. They were incapable of planning. Where we could have had abundance they have created poverty; people are dying of cold and very nearly of starvation; the women suffer and the children are wasting away and dying.

Even more deplorable is the way the war is being conducted: meaningless sallies, murderous engagements without results, repeated failures that would discourage the bravest of men. And Paris is being bombarded!

The Government has shown what it is worth – it is massacring us. The safety of Paris calls for a rapid decision. The Government replies to public criticism with threats; it declares that it will maintain ORDER – as Bonaparte did before Sedan.[1]

If the men of the Hôtel de Ville have any patriotism left their duty is to withdraw and to let the people of Paris organize their own liberation. The Municipality or the Commune, whatever one chooses to call it, is the only salvation of the people, their only guarantee against destruction.

For us to join or to participate in the present government would merely be plastering over the cracks and repeating the same disastrous errors. The continuation of this régime means capitulation, and we have learnt at Metz and Rouen that capitulation is sure to be followed not only by famine but by ruin for everyone, ruin and shame. The Army and the National Guard will be taken prisoner and led through the towns of Germany to the insults of the foreigner. Trade will cease, industry will be destroyed and Paris will be crushed under the burden of war taxes. This is what incompetence and treachery are laying in store for us.

---

[1] The defeat by Prussia of an entire French army at Sedan on 1 September 1870 and the capture of Napoleon III brought about the end of the Second Empire.

Will the Great People of '89, who destroy Bastilles and overthrow monarchs, wait in helpless despair while their hearts are frozen by cold and starvation under the very eyes of the enemy?

THE PEOPLE OF PARIS WILL NEVER ACCEPT SUCH SUFFERING AND SHAME. THEY KNOW THAT THERE IS TIME YET, THAT DECISIVE ACTION CAN STILL ENABLE THE WORKERS TO LIVE AND THE WHOLE POPULATION TO FIGHT

GENERAL REQUISITION – FREE RATIONING – ALL-OUT ATTACK

THE POLICY, STRATEGY, ADMINISTRATION OF THE GOVERNMENT OF 4 SEPTEMBER, ALL ALIKE CONTINUATIONS OF THE EMPIRE, ARE CONDEMNED. *MAKE WAY FOR THE PEOPLE! MAKE WAY FOR THE COMMUNE!*

Poster (*L'Affiche rouge*), issued by the Central Committee of the Twenty Arrondissements, calling for the establishment of a Commune, 6 January 1871: *M.P.*, vol. i, pp. 490–1.

Upon the overthrow of Empire street names were altered. Here the rue du 10 Décembre is replaced by the rue du 4 Septembre (the date the Republic was proclaimed).

49

Part Two: Prelude to the Commune – The Surrender of Paris and the National Elections

The period from the end of January to March 1871 was concerned at the national level with the elections for a National Assembly and with the conclusion of the peace treaty with the Prussians. Paris was in effect abandoned, left to its own devices, and was largely in the hands of the National Guard. This body declared its independence of the National Government by electing its own Central Committee to command it (Document 4). As both Documents 4 and 5 show, the main fear was that the newly elected National Assembly, with its monarchist majority, might try to overthrow the Republic, proclaimed by Paris on 4 September 1870 on the news that Napoleon III had been captured by the Prussians at Sedan. The Vigilance Committee movement, after the failure of its attempted uprising (cf. Document 3), now, at the end of February, formed itself into a 'Revolutionary Socialist party' (Document 6). The strength of support for the Republic and for certain social reforms among the working classes in Paris is well illustrated by the letter of a young artisan, a joiner, to his family in the provinces (Document 7) – many Paris working men were of provincial origins.

4 The National Guard meets

The delegates of the National Guard held their General Meeting in the Tivoli-Vauxhall gardens on 24 February, during which they formed themselves into a Central Committee.

They decided to have their statutes printed in large quantities and sold in Paris so that every company could become acquainted with them and discuss them.

When these resolutions had been adopted the following motions were debated and unanimously passed:

1 The National Guard protests through the intermediary of its Central Committee against all attempts at disarmament, and declares that it will resist these attempts by force if necessary.

2 The delegates will submit the following resolution to the headquarters of their respective companies:

50 'At the first signal that the Prussians are entering Paris all Guards pledge

National Guards man a barricade in defence of the Place Vendôme, site of the headquarters of the National Guard. This was one of the few solid barricades erected before the fighting during the last week of the Commune.

themselves to report immediately in arms to their usual assembly point, from which point they will proceed against the invader.'[1]

3 In the present circumstances the National Guard recognizes only those leaders appointed by the National Guardsmen themselves.

A delegate from the Central Committee will be in charge of organizing a centre of operations from each assembly point.

The meeting rose at six o'clock. The Committee then proceeded to the Bastille to pay a tribute to the martyrs of 1830 and 1848.

Report of the meeting of the Paris National Guard to elect
its own Central Committee, 24 February 1871: *Enquête
parlementaire sur l'insurrection du 18 mars*, vol. iii, p. 14.

---

[1] As part of the peace treaty between France and Prussia the Prussian army was permitted to make a ceremonial entry into Paris along the Champs-Élysées. The National Guard at first thought of opposing this by force, but in the end backed down, encouraged by the International, the Trade Union Federation and the Central Committee of the Twenty Arrondissements.

5 The National Guard's objectives

. . . As you know, Citizens, in spite of the ineptitude of the 4 September Government, and even after the signing of the shameful treaty delivering our proud capital to the enemy, the people still would not believe in the odious plot to betray the Republic. Although the facts were staring them in the face they refused to admit that the men responsible for the downfall of the country were anything more than disgracefully incompetent.

The honest, courageous and patriotic people could not believe their government could behave so contemptibly; they did not realize, on 22 January any more than on 31 October,[1] how wary they ought to be of these men who were in fact their bitter enemies.

However, they did realize that to achieve an honourable peace, to rescue our territory intact from the wreckage, they would have to elect a National Assembly of energetic and devoted patriots, men deeply and sincerely committed to republican institutions.

They therefore organized electoral meetings, still confident in the patriotism of the provinces which they believed to be in a state of general uprising, and counting on every Frenchman to do his duty to the country.

Thus your association was formed, with purely electoral objectives, in an attempt to bring together the National Guard in a common endeavour.

But when the remaining illusions vanished and the dreadful machinations of the reactionaries were exposed; when we saw Paris, the heroic and martyred city, slandered and despised by the blackguards who have exploited the people through the ages; when a shameful and hideous peace settlement was rushed through when we could still call upon vast resources and all the energy of desperate men to help us win our liberation; when all the government posts were taken over by men known for their hostility to the Republic; finally, when Paris had to suffer the ultimate humiliation of foreign occupation, then at last it dawned on the innocently trusting people that they could count on no one but themselves to defend their honour and freedom.

This is how the Central Committee acquired its importance; its banner was a rallying point for all those who mourn for our crippled Nation, who have longed for the hour of freedom and the advent of the Republic and who must join forces now to protect her from further attack. . . .

We are an irresistible barrier against all attempts to overthrow the Republic.

---

[1] A reference to the uprisings of those dates during the siege. That of 31 October 1870 nearly resulted in the overthrow of the Government of National Defence; that of 22 January 1871 was put down by troops firing on the crowd before the Hôtel de Ville – the first blood shed between Frenchmen in 1871.

Ours is the perilous honour of defending it; we will not fail in our mission.

Let them call us trouble-makers, creators of dissention and disorder. Our behaviour proves beyond all doubt that these accusations are false. We are obdurate conservatives – our aim is to conserve all forms of liberty for which the Republic stands.

Nothing could be further from our intention than to provoke violent and damaging conflict between citizens. We reach out a fraternal hand to all our fellow-citizens, to all the peoples of the world who are also our brothers. But now that we have won back the right to control our lives we will not part with it. We will no longer put up with alienation, with monarchs, oppressors and exploiters of all kinds who have come to regard their fellow-men as property and who use them for the satisfaction of their criminal instincts.

To each the rights and duties befitting the condition of a free man.

This is our programme which we loudly proclaim for all to hear.

Speech by Georges Arnold, secretary of the National
Guard, on its formation and its objectives, 10 March 1871
(abridged): *E.P.*, vol. iii, pp. 29–30.

Formation of a 'Revolutionary Socialist party'

Resolutions concerning the Vigilance Committees voted
by General Meetings of these Committees on 20 and 23 February 1871

1 The Vigilance Committees of each arrondissement are to reconstitute themselves immediately and are not to include those members whose tendencies are not sufficiently Revolutionary Socialist.
2 All members of Vigilance Committees must endorse the Declaration of Principles voted at the meeting of 19 February 1871, a copy of which will be available at the Central Office to be consulted by the committees.
3 The administrative structure of the Vigilance Committees is to include a permanently staffed office and a proper system of accountancy.
4 Each committee will keep the Central Office informed of its membership, the address of its offices, the times at which they are open and the private address of the Committee Secretary.
5 Members of Vigilance Committees will pay a weekly subscription of 0·25 franc to meet the expenses of the Central Office. The committees will be responsible to the Central Office for the collection of these subscriptions.
6 The Vigilance Committees will try to constitute groups of supporters in whatever form seems appropriate. These groups will pay a small weekly

subscription, thus providing a regular income for the committees over and above the returns from public meetings.

7 At the end of every month the Vigilance Committees will inform the Treasurer of the Central Office of their balance in hand, to be approved by the Chairman and Secretary of the committees. Half of this balance will be handed over to the Treasurer.

8 The Vigilance Committees will strive to bring under their wing all groups in their arrondissements of a recognized Revolutionary Socialist character by including delegates from these groups among their members.

Declaration of Principles

All members of Vigilance Committees declare their allegiance to the Revolutionary Socialist party. They consequently demand and seek to achieve by every means the abolition of the privileges of the bourgeoisie, its elimination as a ruling caste and the advent of the workers to political power. In a word, social equality: no more employers, no more proletariat, no more classes. They consider that work is the sole basis of the social order and that its product should belong entirely to the worker.

In the political sphere they consider that the Republic is more important than majority rule and therefore do not recognize the right of majorities to deny the principle of popular sovereignty either directly, by plebiscite, or indirectly, through an assembly representing these majorities. They will therefore resist, by force if necessary, the formation of a Constituent Assembly or other alleged National Assembly before the foundations of the present social order are radically altered through political and social revolutionary action.

Until this definitive revolution is accomplished the only government of Paris they recognize is the Revolutionary Commune formed by the delegates of Revolutionary Socialist groups of the city. The only national government they recognize is the government of political and social renewal formed by the delegates of revolutionary communes of the country and of the principal workers' centres.

They undertake to fight for these ideas and to propagate them by forming Revolutionary Socialist groups wherever these do not yet exist. These groups are to be federated and linked with the Central Office.

Finally, they will devote their energies to propaganda work for the International Working Men's Association.

Formation by the Vigilance Committees of a
'Revolutionary Socialist party', 20 and 23 February 1871:
Bourgin, *La Guerre de 1870–1871 et la Commune*, p. 182,
reprints the original, now in the Archives Nationales; see
too Archives Historiques de la Guerre, Ly 26 bis.

A craftsman's letter

... Picard[1] says that we are gambling with our lives – very well, we accept the risk. The Republic holds our fate in its hands; to die for its sake and before it does, that is my wish. If my head is to fall you will know that it is for the cause of the people and none other.

Tell the country people that we do not want civil war, but if those bandits try to remove us we will burn Paris down rather than let them defeat us.

We do not want looting or theft, we do not want pomp and ceremony. Here is what we want and nothing else. A united and indivisible Republic; the separation of Church and State; free and compulsory education by lay teachers; the abolition of all permanent armies and every citizen to bear arms, but in his own district, that is, as the National Guard; the abolition of the Sergents de Ville and all coppers including the Gendarmes.

Let those who declared war pay the costs, along with the dirty capitulators who signed the so-called peace.

This is our programme, which may well have succeeded by the time you read this letter, for we are at present masters of the situation and a good part of the troops are on our side.

But anything you read in the newspapers other than what I am telling you now, well, it's all a foul lie; we are not rogues or thieves, we are the people, nothing more, and nothing is above us.

Letter from a young craftsman to his family, 9 March 1871 (abridged): A.H.G., Ve Conseil, dossier 700; reprinted in Rougerie, *Procès des Communards*, pp. 176–77.

---

[1] Minister for Home Affairs in the government at Versailles.

Part Three: The Uprising of 18 March

The attempt by the National Government to disarm the Paris National Guard on Saturday, 18 March was a complete fiasco because the regular army fraternized with the Paris National Guards. Instead of asserting its control over the city the government was forced to flee to the safety of Versailles. The main attack was on the heights of the Buttes de Montmartre (where the Sacré Cœur Church stands today), where 171 of the cannon seized earlier had been gathered. The account in The Times of London (Document 8) was right to remark on the slowness of the French army under General Vinoy in carting the guns away before the population had had time to realize what was going on. Partly because of his mismanagement of this affair Vinoy was superseded as Commander-in-Chief by Marshal MacMahon. The confusion of The Times's correspondent only mirrored the general disarray of forces on both sides. It was a spontaneous uprising in which all the initiative came from the local National Guards. The events at Montmartre, which The Times correspondent missed, led to the main bloodshed of the day, the mob killing of the captured regular General Lecomte and of a retired general disliked for his role in putting down the June 1848 uprising in Paris. The rather fulsome account by a certain Verges d'Esbœufs (Document 9) is one of several contemporary French descriptions; d'Esbœufs was an active member of the Revolutionary Committee in the 17th arrondissement, which included the socialist Benoît Malon.

8 The Times's correspondent reports

The heights of Montmartre being the ground I know best, and where resistance seemed most likely to be made, I hurried off to the Rue Lepic, at the entrance to which I was stopped by a cordon of soldiers of the Line. All along the Boulevard de Clichy and the Boulevard Rochechouart were regiments of the Line drawn up, and pointing to each of the streets leading to the Place St. Pierre and the Buttes of Montmartre was a loaded cannon raking the narrow lanes. A strong guard protected each of these guns, and prevented ingress. While vainly endeavouring to force a way past a General and Staff rode by, followed by a long train of artillery horses, and slipping in between them I got unperceived into the Rue Lepic. This was quite deserted, and the artillery horses clattered up its steep ascents so

*Above, barricade at the junction of the rue d'Allemagne and the rue Sébastopol
spontaneously thrown up by citizens and National Guards on 18 March (the day
this picture was taken) to prevent the army seizing the cannon assembled on the
Buttes de Montmartre. Below, one of the cannon in place, overlooking the city.*

rapidly as to make it difficult on foot to keep pace with them. Passing round the Moulin à la Galette they entered the battery which some weeks ago I had explored by moonlight, and began to tackle on to the guns. I now perceived that several hundred Line soldiers were inside the enclosure, guarding long piles of National Guard rifles which had been captured, and mounting sentry over the guns; red trousers were everywhere guarding every avenue, and it seemed evident that the day, or rather the morning, was won, and that nothing remained but to carry off the cannon triumphantly. Mixing with a gloomy group of women and National Guards out of uniform, I listened to their conversations, and overheard them indignantly denouncing their chiefs, the Government, M. Thiers, and the world in general. The company of National Guards had been surprised in the gray dawn, and had fled, leaving their guns behind them, at the first appearance of the troops. Seeing that there was no apparent chance of any fighting, and that the guard had given up their guns, I hurried to the battery above the Place St. Pierre. This was also in full occupation of the Line; soldiers were busily engaged in levelling the embrasures with pick and shovel, in filling up the trench, and preparing a way to take off the guns, which were still there waiting for the horses. Here, too, were small savage groups of blouses making cynical remarks upon everybody's cowardice, and wondering where the defenders of the guns might be. 'If they had only left them to us to guard,' said a woman, 'they would not have been captured so easily.' It seemed that before daylight a body of troops had stolen upon them from the rear, and the guard had fled, as they did at Galette. The question which arose in one's mind was why, if the guns were captured at half-past 4, they were still on the ground at half-past 8. Where were the horses, and why was precious time being thrown away? Still, never doubting that the game was won by the Government here, too, and hearing that there was fighting going on at Belleville, I hurried off in that direction, and on the way passed the end of the Rue Clignancourt. Looking up it I saw that it was crowded with National Guards, and that a barricade was being thrown up; this in the immediate proximity of the troops I had just left was still more perplexing, but the mouth of the Rue Clignancourt was held by troops of the Line, who would not let me pass. It was only by looking between them that I could see, two or three hundred yards distant, the National Guard making the barricade. Following the Boulevard Rochechouart, I reached the Boulevard Ornano, at the entrance to which a large body of the Line were massed, while they also occupied the balconies and windows on both sides of the street. Finding that they did not obstruct the passage, I entered the Boulevard, and had not gone many yards when I saw approaching in the distance a large column of National Guards, completely blocking the street, and advancing steadily towards the troops. In a twinkling the foot passengers on the pavement, seeing a collision imminent, took refuge in the houses, and for a moment the position on the abandoned pavement was disagreeable; but a National Guard came along shouting, 'N'ayez-pas peur, il n'y a pas de danger,'[1] and I then perceived that in front of the column was a group of soldiers of the Line, shouting and laughing, and, as it seemed, leading them. As soon as they got within 20 or 30 yards of the Line regiment, the soldiers leading the National Guard, and who acted as a sort of screen of protection, shouted 'Vive la République!' This seemed to be the signal for the whole of the regular troops to throw the butts of their rifles in the air, a movement which was responded to by the whole of the National Guards by enthusiastic shouts of 'Vive la Ligne!' and the instantaneous reversal of all their butts. For a moment there was nothing to be seen but the butt-ends of rifles, or to be heard but loud shouts of 'Vive la Ligne!' 'Vive la République!' The soldiers in the balconies and windows, where, I suppose, they had been placed to shoot the Guards, came down and embraced them instead; women shed tears of joy, and talked about their sons and brothers who were sous le drapeau;[2] arms were intertwined, hands wrung, cheeks kissed and all the extreme demonstrations of fraternization to which Frenchmen are prone when they are not shooting at you out of a window. The officers seemed somewhat embarrassed by the episode, but put as good a face upon it as circumstances would admit. There was something intensely exciting in the scene. The uncertainty for a moment whether the men were meeting as friends or enemies, the wild enthusiasm of the shouts of fraternization, the waving of the upturned muskets, the bold reckless women laughing and exciting the men against their officers, all combined to produce a sensation of perplexity not unmingled with alarm at the strange and un-expected turn things were taking. Still Belleville and the Buttes de Chaumont had an especial attraction for me, and leaving the crowd of citizens and soldiers mingled in confusion, I hurried on, turned back pitilessly by cordons of soldiers first at one street and then at another, and only able at length to force a passage under cover of a card which entitled the bearer to distribute the dons patriotiques d'Angleterre.[3] Glad to escape from the curious throng that blocked the avenues near the sentries in every direction, I hurried along the broad road round the park and found the whole place in occupation of the Government troops. Strong bodies were posted on the rugged open spaces where the lawless crowds of these parts love to hold their meetings and park their cannon. All the guns were in possession of the Artillery; the entrenched camp of which we have heard of late was evacuated and occupied; in fact, here, too, the surprise and

---

[1] 'Don't be afraid, there's no danger.'
[2] 'Serving with the colours'.
[3] 'The patriotic gift of the English', a reference to the funds collected in Britain after the siege to relieve the suffering in Paris.

discomfiture of the National Guards seemed to have been complete. Turning up one of the by-streets which leads into the heart of Belleville I found I had passed the last sentry. The Regulars were no longer visible, the street was deserted except by muttering groups, windows were stealthily opened, people peered timidly from the cracks of doors, and watched a solitary stranger with evident suspicion and dislike. At last, in a narrow lane, I came suddenly upon a sentry. No Regular he, but a full-blown insurgent. '*On ne passe pas, citoyen*',[1] said he gruffly, 'at least without arms; if you want to pass, go and put on your uniform and bring your musket, then you may pass.' 'Why, do you intend to fight?' '*Sacrebleu*, do you suppose we are going to allow these *canaille* to take our cannon without firing a shot? Wait here if you wish to see how we can fight.' At this moment his face changed, and turning round I perceived a company of Regulars advancing straight towards us. At the same moment a number of National Guards rushed to their arms and closed round the sentry I had been speaking to. The moment was critical. Was there a doorway handy, and had either side pluck enough to fire at fifty paces? Such were the ideas which flashed upon one at the moment. At that moment a door opened slowly, and without asking leave I dashed in, nearly upsetting a young woman whose curiosity had induced her to peep from behind it. It was a useless precaution. Warily re-opening the chink we looked out, and lo, the fire-eating sentry threw his butt in the air and shouted wildly '*Vive la Ligne!*' Then all the National Guards who surrounded him threw their butts in the air and followed his lead, and the company turned their butts up, but said nothing; both sides were evidently prepared to do anything rather than shed each others' blood; but whether the party of order had fraternised with the party of disorder, or vice versa, was somewhat difficult to make out. I suspected the latter, for the officer in command got very red, and called his men back; he had apparently intended to pass through the street, but finding his men thus disposed he called out, '*Allons, mes enfants, nous allons faire un petit tour.*'[2] Some of his men followed him, but others lingered with the National Guard, who were overwhelming them with felicitations upon their brotherly conduct. Finally the captain got his men together, doing so in an uneasy, timid manner, and I determined to follow them. Before doing so, however, I was induced by a sudden movement on the part of the National Guard to remain a moment, and to my surprise half-a-dozen picks were produced, and before the Line were out of sight the first half-dozen stones of a barricade were laid. Running after the company of the Line, I passed along a narrow street deserted by every one, and suddenly came out upon the open space in front of the *Mairie* of Belleville. Here was drawn up a *peloton* of cavalry, about two companies of

---

[1] 'You can't come past here, citizen.'

[2] 'Let's go, men, we'll go a different way.'

the Line, three mitrailleuses, and a battery of artillery. Here, too, were small groups of spectators commenting on the proceedings. Presently a Line company was forced back so as to enclose the group in which I happened to find myself; instantly there was whispered fraternization. 'What canaille all your officers are,' said one. 'True,' said a soldier; 'there is one that deserves to be shot, but that man next to him is a brave man; he is a lieutenant.' 'Ah,' said a woman, 'they are sacré gredins, all of them, especially the old ones. They can fight against French fathers of families, but not against Prussians. Are you not ashamed of coming to fire upon us?' 'Who said we were going to fire upon you?' replied the soldier. 'Look,' said one bystander to another, loud enough for the soldiers to hear, 'how uneasily these poor fellows act the vilain métier they are called on to perform. Brave garçons, is it not a pity they should be forced to do such dirty work?' 'We have not done any dirty work yet. Do you think I will fire on a Frenchman? Am I not a Frenchman? Have I not twice been taken prisoner by the Prussians, once at Sedan and once at Dijon? Why, then, should I fire upon my countrymen?' I only give this, as nearly word for word as I can remember, as a specimen of the conversation I heard all round me. Just then my curiosity was excited by a chinking noise, which seemed to come from beyond a group of several hundred soldiers. Mounting on a large stone, so as to look over them, I observed a number of National Guards engaged in making a barricade within three yards of the first line of soldiers. The sight was so astounding that I could not help asking a gentlemanlike-looking officer near me why it was allowed. He flushed up a little angrily, and said that it was a dangerous place to be in, and still more a dangerous time to ask questions which did not concern me, and to which, therefore, it was not necessary for him to reply. Thus snubbed, and more puzzled than ever, I retired into a small tavern. There were not above a dozen persons present altogether on the little Place besides the military, and there was constant passing in and out of the Mairie. What seemed strange was that although the horses were harnessed to the guns there was no attempt made to take them for nearly an hour. It was almost 11 when the column began to move off, leaving the infantry behind. I followed it back to the Buttes de Chaumont, visiting on my way the barricade of which I had seen the first stone laid, and which had now grown to considerable dimensions by reason of the rule which is enforced that every passer must place a stone, a pile of which is placed for the purpose on each side of the street. Some large carts had been also brought, and new barricades were springing up in every direction. I followed the artillery column till they came to a sudden halt by the side of the Parc de Chaumont, and, for some inexplicable reason, remained there doing nothing. Why these guns had not been carried off hours before remains still a mystery. While wondering what they were going to do next I was startled by a shot, and, running in the 61 direction, found a swarm of National Guards making another barricade with carts and stones, and some Regulars retiring towards the guns. After this all was still for some time. It was now midday, and the whole affair wore a most strange and incomprehensible aspect to one not brought up to make barricades, and afraid to be too inquisitive. Seeing that at all events there was not likely to be any fighting here, I went back to Montmartre. What a change had come over the spirit of its dream since I had seen it four hours before! . . . There was not a red trouser to be seen, excepting here and there a straggler making a fraternal speech to an admiring audience, telling them how he would rather shoot himself than shoot a countryman; what cowards and *canaille* his officers were, etc. Instead of a Government blocking up every street as was the case in the morning, a hostile cannon was now looking down every street; where there had been a cordon of soldiers there was now a cordon of rebellious National Guards, who, flushed with an almost bloodless victory, were swaggering about super-intending the construction of barricades and making life a burden to any one who had not a red stripe down his leg. These streets, so deserted in the morning, excepting here and there a slinking warrior, were now swarming with them, drums were beating, bugles blowing, and all the din of victory. Lower down a captain of Chasseurs had ordered his men to fire. The words were no sooner out of his mouth than he fell riddled with balls, whether from his men or his enemies is not yet known; but several shots were fired from windows at the time and a dozen or more men of the Line were killed or wounded, so it is possible that the officer was shot also by the National Guards. A couple of the horses dragging a gun were also killed, and were just moved away as I passed. The whole of the Line had upon this taken to their heels, and the whole region was in absolute and undisputed possession of the insurgents.

Account in *The Times* of London of the events on the Right Bank on the morning of 18 March: *The Times*, 20 March 1871, abridged.

9 *An eye-witness account*

The women and children were swarming up the hill-side in a compact mass; the artillerymen tried in vain to fight their way through the crowd, but the waves of people engulfed everything, surging over the cannon-mounts, over the ammunition waggons, under the wheels, under the horses' feet, paralysing the action of the riders who spurred on their mounts in vain. The horses reared and lunged forward, their sudden movement clearing the crowd, but the space was filled at once by a backwash created by the surging multitude.

Like breakers, the first rows of the crowd came crashing on to the batteries, repeatedly flooding them with people.

The artillerymen and cavalrymen of the train were holding their own with brave determination. The cannons had been entrusted to them and they made it a point of honour to defend them.

At that moment the National Guard arrived; they had great difficulty in breaking through the crowd who were obstinately clinging to the wheels.

The women especially were crying out in fury: 'Unharness the horses! Away with you! We want the cannons! We shall have the cannons!'

The artillerymen could see, beyond the ocean of people, the gleaming steel of the bayonets; in the face of such resistance all advance was impossible, but they still did not falter.

Soldiers who had deserted their regiments shouted to them to surrender, but they stayed in the saddle and continued to spur their horses on furiously.

A National Guardsman who had managed to reach the scene of the action climbed on to a milestone and shouted: 'Cut the traces!'

The crowd let out a great cheer. The women closest to the cannons, to which they had been clinging for half an hour, took the knives that the men passed down to them from hand to hand. They cut through the harnesses.

The same National Guardsman now shouted: 'Open up the ranks! Spur on the horses! Let them through!'

The manœuvre was carried out amid joyful laughter and cheering.

The artillerymen were carried off by their mounts and found themselves cut off from the guns and surrounded by groups of people inviting them to fraternize.

They were offered flasks of wine and meat rolls.

They too were hungry and thirsty. They were soon won over to the side of the rebels.

The cannons had been retaken. The cannons were in the hands of the people.

But at this point only a few companies had gone over to the other side. The main force of the brigade on top of the Buttes, the Gendarmes, the Police, the cavalry, and in particular a battalion of the 88th led by an enterprising lieutenant-colonel still threatened Montmartre.

General Lecomte was no doubt still confident of victory. . . .

He occupied the summit of the Buttes, covering the approach of the sentry-post of the Rue des Rosiers captured that night from the National Guard.

The Guards who had been taken prisoner and the soldiers who had refused to shoot were locked up in the post.

63

General Lecomte was in command of considerable forces: various police units, light infantry and infantry of the line. He was not aware, as we said before, of the developments on the hill-side but he had heard the growing noise of the revolt.

Not that this caused him any concern. He assumed that General Susbielle and his reserve brigade would be ordered by the Commander-in-Chief, General Vinoy, to launch an attack on the Federals from the back, while Lecomte himself would fire on them from the front.

He had taken the precaution of placing sentries in positions where they might warn him of the arrival of the rebels; he awaited the crowd confidently.

He was undoubtedly a brave soldier and this he was proving. When his sentries fell back and announced that the Federals were approaching, he declared: 'We shall clean them up!'

At this point the 79th Federal Battalion was sighted, coming to a halt at the right of the Solferino tower.[1] It was headed by two officers named Lalande and Coulon. They stepped forward from the ranks to parley; Lalande, a captain, had stuck his handkerchief on the end of his sword.

The National Guard all raised their rifle-butts in the air and awaited the result of the confrontation. . . .

At that moment General Lecomte appeared.

It must be pointed out that up to then no officer of the light infantry had given orders to fire.

The General must have realized the battalion was unreliable, so he came to take command of it himself.

The crowd of women and children massed at the entrance of the Rue Muller saw that the General was about to give orders to fire. They gave way to a spontaneous movement and, instead of fleeing, threw themselves in front of the infantrymen, shouting, 'Don't fire!'

The General, his voice resounding clearly above the noise, ordered: 'Make ready to fire!'

The soldiers obeyed. The crowd halted.

'Shoulder arms!'

Rifle-butts were pressed against shoulders, barrels were lowered. A shiver went through the crowd, but no one moved.

A brief but profound silence, then the shout: 'Fire!'

An agonizing suspense. The Federals made ready to avenge the crowd should the troops fire. But the soldiers refused to obey.

One rifle was raised, then ten, then a hundred, as though the shadow of death that had been hovering over the crowd had suddenly flown away and spared them.

[1] At the top of the Buttes de Montmartre.

The General sternly rebuked the infantrymen; he pointed a revolver at them and threatened to blow the brains out of anyone who refused to fire.

The Federals saw him and heard his words. He repeated the order to fire three times. He was even overheard to say the following words: 'Fire at least once for the sake of honour!'

Nothing could move the soldiers or provoke them to action; they remained impassive.

The General was beside himself with rage. 'Are you going to surrender to that scum?', he cried contemptuously.

A soldier then replied in these very words: 'That is exactly what we want to do.' And he threw down his rifle.

At that point Lalande, the Federal Captain who had come to parley, placed his hand on the General's shoulder and said: 'It is you who must surrender!'

The General struggled and shouted, not to the infantrymen any more but to the Police and the Gendarmes: 'Defend me! Fire! Fire!'

But the infantrymen, the Federals, the crowd seized the Gendarmes, disarmed them and took some of them prisoner. Eighty of them were held in the mairie.[1]

The General gave in. He realized the full meaning of the situation. His faith in military power, his contempt for the people, his hopes and ambitious dreams, all had vanished in the face of stark reality: he had been taken prisoner.

Supposed eye-witness account of the events in Montmartre on 18 March 1871: d'Esbœufs, *La Vérité sur La Commune par un ancien proscrit*, pp. 232–40, abridged.

---

[1] Each of the Paris arrondissements had its own mairie, the local town hall, and maire, the mayor. In addition there was a Mayor of Paris and a town hall, the Hôtel de Ville.

Part Four: From Revolt to the Proclamation of the Commune 18–28 March 1871

The ten days following the uprising of Saturday, 18 March, were occupied, from the revolutionaries' viewpoint, with trying to legalize the occupation of the Hôtel de Ville by holding municipal elections. These finally took place on 26 March and the Paris Commune was formally proclaimed on Tuesday 28 March. During this period several interpretations of the meaning of the revolt were put forward, the most revolutionary and socialist one being that of the delegates appointed by the National Guard Central Committee to the official paper of all French governments, the Journal Officiel *(Document 10). Marx quoted part of this document in his essay,* The Civil War in France, *written just after the fall of the Commune. The Paris section of the International, after some hesitation, finally came out in favour of the National Guard and its revolution (Document 11). The manifesto of the International was mainly the work of the bronze-worker Albert Theisz, who became head of the Post Office during the Commune, and of the stone-carver Antoine Demay, both of whom were elected to the Commune. Local electoral committees also drew up their lists of candidates and declarations of principles. That for the 11th arrondissement (Document 12), to the east on the Right Bank and one of the most revolutionary districts, strongly expressed the view that the Republic implied social reform and greater control over the State by its citizens. Five of its seven candidates were elected.*

The formal proclamation of the Commune from the steps of the Hôtel de Ville was a dazzling ceremony that moved all observers. The account given here (Document 13), written by Jules Vallès for his paper, Le Cri du Peuple, *emphasizes the festive nature of the day.*

10 Contemporary view of the uprising

The Revolution of 18 March

The reactionary newspapers continue to mislead public opinion by deliberately distorting the political events that have taken place in the capital in the last three days. They have published the most blatant slander, the most outrageous accusations against the brave and disinterested men who have taken on the heavy responsibility of defending the Republic in the face of great danger.

To the cheers of the people of Paris, the Commune is proclaimed from the balcony of the Hôtel de Ville, 28 March 1871 – 'a festival of dazzling simplicity', one observer wrote.

Impartial historians cannot fail to do these men justice and recognize that the Revolution of 18 March is a new and important step in the march of progress.

Proletarians whose names were unknown yesterday but who will soon be world-famous, brave men moved by a profound love of justice and human rights and by a boundless devotion to France and the Republic have resolved to deliver the country from the invader and defend our threatened freedom. They will be praised for these actions by their contemporaries and by future generations.

The proletarians of the capital, faced with the incompetence and treachery of the ruling classes, have realized that the hour has come for them to save the situation by taking public affairs into their own hands.

They have exercised the power conferred on them by the people with a moderation and wisdom that cannot be praised too highly.

They have remained unruffled by the provocations of the enemies of the Republic and vigilant in the presence of the invader.

They have shown extreme selflessness and devotion. As soon as they came to power they urged the people of Paris to organize electoral meetings for the immediate formation of a communal municipality to whom they would abdicate their briefly held powers. Never in history has there been a provisional government so eager to hand over its mandate to representatives elected by universal suffrage.

It is a subject of wonder that their disinterested, honest and democratic behaviour could possibly deserve such disgracefully unjust treatment by the Press; that slander, insults and outrage could thus be heaped on respectable citizens whose actions have until now been worthy only of praise and admiration.

Must the friends of Humanity, the defenders of Justice, whether in victory or defeat, always be the victims of lies and slander?

Will the workers, who produce everything and receive nothing in return, who endure poverty in the midst of wealth which they have produced by the sweat of their brow, always be subjected to abuse?

Will they never be able to work towards their emancipation without provoking a chorus of invectives?

How can the bourgeoisie, their elders, who achieved emancipation more than three-quarters of a century ago and preceded them on the revolutionary path, not understand that today it is the turn of the proletariat to be emancipated?

The disasters that have befallen France through the political incompetence and moral and intellectual decrepitude of the bourgeoisie ought to be proof enough that their time is up, that the task that was theirs in '89 has now been accomplished. If they do not give way to the workers they must at least allow them to achieve their own social emancipation.

In the present catastrophic situation we cannot get by without the participation of the whole population. Why then do they persist so stubbornly and with such dangerous lack of foresight in refusing the proletariat their rightful share of emancipation?

Why do they continually challenge their basic rights? Why do they employ all their powers and resources in resisting the efforts of the working class to seek fulfilment?

Why do they constantly threaten the achievements of the human mind
represented by the Great French Revolution?

If since 4 September the ruling class had allowed the needs and aspirations of the people to be freely expressed, if they had simply granted the workers their basic rights and the exercise of all forms of freedom, if they had allowed them to develop their faculties fully, exercise all their rights and satisfy their needs, if they had not preferred the destruction of the country to the certain victory of the Republic in Europe we would not be where we are, we would have avoided this catastrophe.

The proletariat, faced with a constant threat to its rights, a total denial of all its legitimate aspirations, along with the imminent destruction of the country and of all its hopes, has realized that it is its imperative duty and absolute right to take its destiny in its own hands by seizing political power.

Revolution was the proletariat's answer to the senseless, criminal provocation of a reckless government that did not hesitate to unleash civil war while under foreign invasion and occupation.

The authorities hoped to induce the army to march against the people, but it refused to attack them; instead it held out a fraternal hand to its brothers and joined forces with them.

Let the blame for the bloodshed – which is always to be deplored – fall upon the instigators of civil war, the enemies of the people who for nearly half a century have been the cause of domestic strife and national disaster.

Though briefly interrupted, the march of progress will now continue unhindered and the proletariat will achieve its emancipation in spite of everything.

Contemporary socialist interpretation of 18 March:
editorial in the *Journal Officiel de la République Française*,
21 March 1871.

The International supports the Commune

FRENCH REPUBLIC
LIBERTY EQUALITY FRATERNITY
International Working Men's Association
Federal Council of Paris Sections
Federation of Trade Unions

Fellow-workers,

A long series of failures, a catastrophe that threatens to ruin our country completely, this is the situation France has inherited from the men who have governed her up to now.

Have we lost all ability to pull ourselves out of this shameful state? Have we fallen so low that we will submit to the hypocritical tyrants who 69

Association Internationale

DES TRAVAILLEURS

CONSEIL FÉDÉRAL DES SECTIONS PARISIENNES

Chambre Fédérale des Sociétés ouvrières

The heading of Document 11 (see previous page).

betrayed us to the enemy? Is there nothing left to do but destroy ourselves once and for all by provoking civil war?

Recent events have shown that the people of Paris are strong, and we are convinced that fraternal understanding will soon prove that they are wise as well.

The principle of authority has proved incapable of bringing back order to the streets and restoring production in the workshops; by its impotence it has negated itself.

The lack of solidarity of interests has led to general ruin and social strife. *Liberty, equality and solidarity must be the new foundations on which we will restore order and reorganize labour, the essential condition of order.*

Fellow-workers,

The Communal Revolution is founded on these principles; it eliminates all causes of conflict in the future. Do you hesitate to give it your full support?

The independence of the Commune will mean a freely discussed contract which will put an end to class conflict and bring about social equality.

We have fought for the emancipation of the working class; the Commune will bring it about, for its function is to enable every citizen to defend his rights, to have effective control over those to whom he has entrusted his interests and to participate in the progressive implementation of social reforms.

The autonomy of the individual communes is a guarantee that they will not assert their rights in an oppressive manner; it is a confirmation of the Republic in its highest form.

Fellow-workers,

We have fought and we have learned to suffer in defence of our egalitarian principles; we cannot turn back now that we can help to lay the foundations
70 of the new social structure.

What are our demands?

The co-operative organization of credit, exchange and production to enable the worker to receive the full value of his labour.

Free, secular and complete education.

The right to assemble and to form associations. The absolute freedom of the Press and of the individual.

Municipal control of the Police, the armed forces, public health, statistics, etc.

We have been taken in by our rulers, who have fooled us by alternately cajoling and repressing the various factions, exploiting their antagonism to retain power.

Today the people of Paris have become aware; they no longer want to be treated like irresponsible children. When they vote in the municipal elections (resulting from a movement created by the people themselves) they will bear in mind that the same principles that govern groups and associations must also preside over the whole of society. Just as they would refuse an administrator or president imposed on them from outside, so they will reject a mayor or a prefect imposed by a government alien to their aspirations.

The people will assert their right, which is higher than the vote of any assembly, to remain masters in their own city and to appoint the municipal representatives of their choice without seeking to impose them on others.

We are convinced that on Sunday, 26 March, the people of Paris will make it a point of honour to vote for the Commune.

Manifesto of the Paris branch of the First International supporting the principle of elections for the Commune, 23 March 1871: *M.P.*, vol. ii, pp. 52–3.

Election poster

FRENCH REPUBLIC
LIBERTY   EQUALITY   FRATERNITY
Statement of Principles
of the Republican, Democratic and Socialist Central Electoral
Committee of the 11th Arrondissement of the City of Paris

Preliminary Statement

All members of the Republican, Democratic and Socialist Central Electoral Committee of the 11th Arrondissement endorse the following Statement of Principles.

General Principles

The Revolution is the march of the peoples of the world for equal rights and duties. In the Democratic and Social Republic this equality becomes a reality. Solidarity must reign among all men. The law must be the progressive embodiment of universal justice. The people must assert the rights and sovereignty that belong to them by birth. The Republic is the only political régime where this sovereignty can be exercised; therefore no majority may decide to replace it by any other form of government. If this were ever to take place it would mean no less than suicide for the people and enslavement for future generations, along with the complete destruction of our natural, legitimate and inalienable rights, which cannot be impeded or restricted:

(1) The right to live; (2) Individual freedom; (3) Freedom of thought; (4) Freedom to assemble and associate; (5) Freedom of speech, of the Press and of all forms of expression; (6) Free elections.

The violation or attempted violation of any one of these rights is legitimate grounds for insurrection. The Democratic and Social Republic should not and does not recognize any form of monarchy, since it believes in the fellowship of the people of all lands as individuals.

Practical Organization

Politics

The State is the people governing themselves through a National Assembly composed of representatives elected by universal, organized and direct suffrage and subject to removal. The people reserve the right to discuss and ratify all institutions and fundamental laws.

Work, Production and Distribution

The whole system of work should be reorganized. Since the aim of life is the limitless development of our physical, intellectual and moral capacities, property is and must only be the right of each one of us to share (to the extent of his individual contribution) in the collective fruit of labour which is the basis of social wealth.

The Nation must provide for those unable to work.

Public Offices (Responsibility)

The officials of the Republic must be responsible at every level for all their actions. All public, national or communal offices should be temporary, elective and accessible to all, subject to a test of ability. All posts are to be remunerated.

The plurality of functions is an offence against the entire Nation or one of its members and will be subject to the severest penalties.

National Defence

It is the duty of all citizens without distinction to defend the national
territory.

Permanent armies will be abolished.

Justice and the Judiciary

Justice should be available to all; it will therefore be free for both defending and prosecuting parties.

All misconduct will be punished proportionately to the extent and consequences of the damage caused.

The jury system will be instituted in all courts.

Human life shall be considered inviolable, and no one shall be allowed to offend against it except in self-defence.

The aim of the penal system shall be the reform of the criminal.

Education

Education should be social. Secular and compulsory elementary education must be universal. Secondary and specialized education will be available to men and women citizens free of charge, on the basis of competitive and ordinary examinations.

Freedom of thought is the natural right of every individual; the various forms of worship will therefore be the entire responsibility of those who practise them. The separation of the churches and the State must be total. It is forbidden to practise any form of worship in public.

Taxation

The burdensome and vexatious fiscal system of numerous different taxes collected in a multiplicity of ways must be abolished. State revenue will be ensured by the levy of a single, progressive tax on all citizens in the form of an insurance premium. This tax will be collected at a local level and will be based on annual income. Each individual commune will control its share of the tax and will be responsible for its collection.

These are, in brief, the principles to which we are committed. We now call for the necessary reforms and political, legislative, financial and administrative measures to carry them into effect.

We look forward to a future where every citizen will exercise his rights to the full and be conscious of his duties, where there will be no more oppressors or oppressed, no class distinctions among citizens and no barriers between the peoples of different nations.

Since the family is the primary form of association, all families will join together to form a greater family, the Nation, and all nations will unite in a superior, collective entity, Humanity.

Poster displayed during the elections to the Commune:
M.P., vol. ii, pp. 84–5.

13 The proclamation of the Commune

THE FESTIVE DAY

The Commune has been proclaimed.

The Commune has emerged from the electoral urn, triumphant, sovereign and armed.

The men elected by the people of Paris have entered the Hôtel de Ville that once resounded with the drums of Santerre and the rifle-fire of 22 January.[1] They have taken up residence in the square where the blood once shed for the honour of the Nation and the dignity of Paris has been dried by the dust of our victorious battalions.

We vow that the drums of Santerre will never roll again, nor the rifles gleam from the windows of our Communal Hôtel de Ville. Never again will the Place de Grève be stained with blood.

The Commune has been proclaimed.

The artillery thunders a salute from the quays; the grey smoke is gilded by the sun. A crowd has gathered to greet the triumphal procession; men wave their hats and women their handkerchiefs while from the barricades the cannons humbly lower their bronze muzzles lest they threaten the joyful onlookers.

In the shade of the dark building, whose clock has struck so many hours that have turned into centuries, witnessed so many events that have now become history, below the windows crowded with respectful attendants, the National Guard march past, cheering with confident and proud enthusiasm.

On the platform stand the men elected by the people – good men with strong, trustworthy faces – and above them the bust of the Republic, white marble against red drapes, calmly looks down on the gleaming forest of bayonets flecked with the brilliant colours of flags and pennants. And above all this the hum of the city, the flourish of brass and the thud of drums, the salvoes and the cheers.

The Commune is proclaimed by a revolutionary, patriotic celebration, a day of peace and joy, excitement and solemnity, splendour and merriment worthy of the days lived by the men of '92. This is our consolation for twenty years of Empire and six months of defeat and treachery.

The people of Paris, armed and proudly erect, hail the Commune which has saved them from the shame of surrender and the indignity of a Prussian victory. It will make them free as they have made it victorious.

If only the Commune had been proclaimed on 31 October! No matter

74   [1] See note 1, p. 52, above.

Jules Vallès, founder of the revolutionary paper, Le Cri du Peuple. *Vallès was one of the young revolutionary Left Bank journalists who had bitterly attacked Napoleon III in the 1860s.*

now. Dead of Buzenval,[1] victims of 22 January, at last you are avenged!

The Commune has been proclaimed. Battalions pour forth spontaneously from the streets, quays and boulevards with a flourish of bugles and a drum-beat that echoes through the streets, stirring every heart. They have come to cheer and salute the Commune, to stage a grand civic review in its honour and in defiance of Versailles. They march on, bearing arms, towards the suburbs, their joyous sound spreading through the great beehive of the city.

The Commune has been proclaimed.

Today is the festive wedding day of the Idea and the Revolution.

Soldier-citizens, the Commune we have acclaimed and married today must tomorrow bear fruit; we must take our place once more, still proud and now free, in the workshop and at the counter.

After the poetry of triumph, the prose of work.

Account by Jules Vallès, the revolutionary journalist, of
the proclamation of the Paris Commune on 28 March:
Le Cri du Peuple, 30 March 1871.

---

[1] The last, and pointless, battle of the siege, in which the National Guard was used for the first and only time.

Part Five: The Commune – Popular Opinion

In its first proclamation (Document 14) the newly elected Commune tried to appeal to all sections of republican opinion. It emphasized the municipal nature of Paris's revolution, stressed that the city was simply claiming its local franchise. The issue of back rents was one that united the working classes with the lower bourgeoisie. By cancelling payments for the last three quarters, covering the period of the siege, the Commune granted a demand that had been strongly pressed by tenants' associations and the majority of the population ever since the end of the war. It was the National Assembly's refusal to take any such action that had alienated much of moderate opinion in Paris from the government at Versailles. 'The mass of Parisian tenants, merchants, embarrassed in their affairs, small rentiers who have been ruined, clerks out of place, as well as workpeople out of work, awoke full of joy on the 29th when they read that three-quarters of their rents were "remitted"', reported The Times's correspondent on 3 April. The promised decree on overdue bills (échéances or promissory notes), which was the other outstanding legacy from the siege, took the Commune much longer to settle. By the time the Commune finally decided to grant a three-year delay on payment, much of middle-class opinion had swung against the revolution.

Control of the National Guard had been the actual point on which the dispute between Paris and the government at Versailles had centered. The events of 18 March meant that power now lay in the hands of the National Guard, and the Commune had no choice other than to ratify this. But disputes between the National Guard's Central Committee and the Commune soon arose, the former body claiming that it alone should be responsible for the war effort. The meeting of the National Guard Central Committee on 23 April (Document 15) was only one of several at which its members, particularly Édouard Moreau, argued that since the National Guard had made the revolution of 18 March it should continue to lead it. The declaration of the Central Committee on 5 April (Document 16) at the outbreak of the civil war is noticeable for the emphasis it placed on a social interpretation of the war.

Ever since the revolution of 18 March the bourgeoisie had been demanding a statement of principles, and some of the revolutionary papers also called on the Commune to issue a programme. The question at issue was whether the Commune should act purely as a municipal government of Paris, or as a revolutionary government of the whole of France. The Declaration to the French People (Document 17) – adopted by the Commune with hardly any discussion – was

Triumphant, Republican France holds aloft the banner of the Social Revolution.

largely drafted by Pierre Denis, a Proudhonist journalist. It accordingly interprets the Commune mainly in federalist terms; Paris was claiming its municipal rights and other local governments throughout France were invited to do the same. The issue of decentralization had been debated in the last years of the Empire, and had the Declaration been published before the outbreak of civil war, Paris might have expected some sympathy on this score. But it appeared too late, and the Versailles police seized most of the copies which got out of Paris. Régère was right when he maintained in the debate on the Declaration that the Commune's only admissible programme was 'our acts and our decrees'. Nevertheless the tone of the document 77 *changes at the end – possibly Vallès or Malon intervened to give it a more revolutionary conclusion.*

The civil war meant that the Commune was caught between its own revolutionary principle of local autonomy and the need for central organization. Its second Delegate of War, Louis-Nathaniel Rossel, a young regular officer who had joined the Commune in the hope that Paris would restart the war against the Prussians, resigned after only nine days in office, his military training making intolerable to him the confusion of the Commune's attempt to manage its war effort (Document 18).

14 The Commune's first decree

PARIS COMMUNE

Citizens,

Your Commune has been formed.

The voters of 26 March have given their approval to the victorious Revolution.

The cowardly aggressors who wielded power had you by the throat, but you have risen in self-defence and have ousted a government that tried to dishonour you by subjecting you to monarchical rule.

At present the criminals whom you did not even seek to punish are abusing your generosity by fostering a hot-bed of monarchist conspiracy at the very gates of the city. They are planning to unleash civil war; no form of corruption or complicity is too base for them; they have even dared to go begging for foreign support.

We expose these loathsome intrigues to the judgment of France and the world.

Citizens,

The institutions you have just created for yourselves are a guarantee against your aggressors.

You are masters of your own lives. Strengthened by your support, your newly elected representatives will remedy the disastrous situation created by the fallen powers. Industry was threatened, work had come to a halt and trade was paralysed, but now our economy will receive a powerful boost.

This very day the awaited decision on rents will be taken.

Tomorrow we will come to a decision on overdue bills.

All public services will be restored and organized on a more rational basis.

The National Guard, from now on the only armed force of the city, will
78 be reorganized without delay.

These will be our first actions.

To ensure the victory of the Republic, the representatives of the people ask only for your confidence and support.

As for them, they will do their duty.

The first decree issued by the Paris Commune, 29 March 1871: *J.O.*, 30 March 1871.

Meeting of the Central Committee of the National Guard

. . . *Moreau* emphasizes the need for the Central Committee to renew its ideological links with the National Guard and to return to its revolutionary role. He demands that we establish some form of control over the Commune. We ought to reorganize a National Assembly, inform it of our actions and demand that it entrusts us with certain powers. We must make the Commune recognize the Central Committee's rights of control. It is essential to have an efficient administration; we must demand its complete reorganization.

The Commune ought to think in terms of encircling Versailles by the revolutionary movement.

He again emphasizes the need to bring out a newspaper.

Rousseau points out that for reasons of protocol delegates of the Central Committee cannot be admitted to the Ministry of War.

Moreau maintains that political considerations should override questions of protocol. The war of attrition we are being subjected to is eroding the Revolution.

Lacord sees no reason why the Central Committee should not have a representative at the Ministry of War; it would thus gain access to essential information. He stipulates however that the representative report daily to the Central Committee.

Rousseau does not think Moreau is suitable for the post at the Ministry.

Prudhomme protests that certain members of the Central Committee have taken up governmental posts without the Committee's consent, but Citizen Moreau has asked for the Committee's approval on all occasions. The important thing is to make sure that Citizen Moreau represents the point of view of the Central Committee in all matters.

Moreau replies that he is a member of the Central Committee and a revolutionary; he will be in a position to protest on behalf of the Central Committee whenever the Ministry is guilty of mismanagement.

Lacord asks that a complaint be addressed to the Commune about Cluseret's mismanagement of affairs.

79

Baroud thinks such a complaint would be turned against the Central Committee, and that the Commune would be all the more disposed to trust Cluseret. He insists on the need to be represented at the War Ministry. *Castioni* agrees.

Rousseau defends the War Commission; they realize what Cluseret is worth and have asked the Central Committee to take over the leadership of the movement. . . .

Report of a meeting of the Central Committee of the
National Guard during the Commune, 23 April 1871
(abridged): *E.P.*, vol. iii, pp. 135–6.

16 *Declaration by the Central Committee of the National Guard*

The Central Committee of the Republican Federation of the National Guard has just issued the following proclamation to the people of Paris:

Citizens,

It is the same old story: the criminals are trying to escape punishment by committing one last crime that will terrify the people into silence.

A handful of perjurers, traitors, perverters and murderers are seeking to drown justice in a blood-bath.

Civil war was their last hope of success and now they have unleashed it – a thousand curses upon them!

Citizens of Paris, the great days of sublime courage and heroism have returned! The welfare of the country and the future of the whole world are in your hands. The generations to come will either praise you or condemn you.

Workers, make no mistake – this is all-out war, a war between parasites and workers, exploiters and producers. If you are tired of vegetating in ignorance and poverty; if you want your children to grow up to enjoy the fruits of their labour rather than be some sort of animal reared for the factory or the battlefield, increasing some exploiter's fortune by the sweat of their brow or shedding their blood for a tyrant; if you no longer want your daughters, whom you cannot raise and care for as you wish, to be instruments of pleasure for the aristocracy of money; if you no longer want poverty and debauchery to drive men into the police force and women into prostitution; finally, if you want justice to reign, workers, use your intelligence, arise! Let your strong hands crush the loathsome forces of reaction!

Citizens of Paris, tradesmen, industrial workers, shopkeepers, intel-
80 lectuals, all of you who work and who earnestly search for a solution to

social problems, the Central Committee entreats you to work together for a better world. Let the destiny of the Nation and its eternal genius be your inspiration.

The Central Committee is convinced that the heroic population of Paris will win immortal fame and regenerate the world.

Long live the Republic! Long live the Commune!

Declaration by the Central Committee of the National
Guard at the first attack (2 April) by the Versailles troops,
5 April 1871: *J.O.*, 7 April 1871.

Declaration to the French People

FRENCH REPUBLIC

LIBERTY   EQUALITY   FRATERNITY

PARIS COMMUNE

DECLARATION TO THE FRENCH PEOPLE

[In the grievous and terrible conflict which once again exposes Paris to the horrors of siege and bombardment, which causes French blood to flow, our brothers, women and children to perish, flattened by shell and grapeshot, public opinion must not be divided, nor the national consciousness confused.

Paris and the whole nation must be informed of the character, the reason and the aim of the Revolution that is taking place, so that the responsibility for the sorrows, the sufferings and the misfortunes of which we are the victims may be laid on those who, having betrayed France and delivered Paris to the foreigner, are now seeking, with blind and cruel obstinacy, to ruin the capital, in order that the twofold witness of their treachery and their crime may be buried alongside the destruction of the Republic and of Liberty.]

It is the duty of the Commune to confirm and ascertain the aspirations and wishes of the people of Paris. The precise character of the movement of the 18th of March is misunderstood and unknown, and is calumniated by the politicians at Versailles.

[Once more] Paris labours and suffers for the whole of France, for whom she prepares by her battles and intellectual, moral, administrative, and economic regeneration, glory and prosperity.

What does she demand?

The recognition and consolidation of the Republic[, the only form of government compatible with the rights of the People and with the free, regular development of society].

81

The absolute independence of the Commune extended at all places in France, thus assuring to each the integrity of its rights and to every Frenchman the full exercise of his faculties and aptitudes as a man, a citizen [and a worker].

The independence of the Commune has no other limits [than the right of all the other communes to an equal autonomy] who are adherents of the contract the association of which ought to secure the unity of France.

The inherent rights of the Commune are:

To vote the Communal budget of receipts and expenses; [to fix and assess] taxes; the direction of local services; the organisation of the magistracy, internal police, and education; the administration of the property belonging to the Commune.

The choice by election or competition, with the responsibility and permanent right of control and revocation, of the Communal magistrates and officials of all classes.

The absolute guarantee of individual liberty, liberty of conscience [and liberty of work].

The permanent intervention of the citizens in Communal affairs by the free manifestation of their ideas and the free defence of their interests; guarantees given for those manifestations by the Commune, which alone is charged with [watching over and ensuring] the free and just exercise of the right of meeting and publicity.

The organisation of urban defence and of the National Guard, which must elect its chiefs and alone watch over the maintenance of order in the city.

Paris wishes nothing more under the head of local guarantees, on the well-understood condition of regaining, in a grand central administration and delegation from the federal communes, the realisation and practice of those same principles.

But [on the strength of] her independence, and profiting by her liberty of action, Paris reserves to herself liberty to bring about as may seem good to her administrative and economic reforms which the people demand, and to create such institutions as may serve to develop and further education, [production,] exchange, and credit; to universalise power and property according to the necessities of the moment, the wishes of those interested, and the data furnished by experience.

Our enemies deceive themselves [and the country] when they accuse Paris of seeking the destruction of French unity, established by the Revolution[, which our fathers acclaimed when they thronged from all corners of old France to the festival of the Federation].

Unity, such has been imposed upon us up to the present by the empire, the monarchy, and parliamentary government, is nothing but centralisation, 82 despotic, unintelligent, arbitrary, and onerous.

Political unity, as desired by Paris, is a voluntary association of all local initiative, the free and spontaneous co-operation of all individual energies with the common object of wellbeing, liberty and security of all.

The Communal Revolution, [begun by popular initiative] on the 18th of March, inaugurated a new era of experimental, positive, and scientific politics.

It [marks the end of the old governmental] and clerical world, of militarism, of bureaucracy, [of exploitation,] of jobbing in monopolies, of privileges, to which the proletariat [owes] its slavery and the country its misfortune and disasters.

[Let this beloved and great country, therefore, deceived by lies and calumnies, be reassured!]

The strife between Paris and Versailles is one of those that cannot be decided by an illusory compromise; the issue should not be doubtful. The victory, fought for with such indomitable energy by the National Guard, will remain [on the side of intelligence (*l'idée*) and of] right.

We appeal to France.

Knowing that Paris in arms possesses as much calmness as courage; [that she maintains] order with as much energy as enthusiasm; [that she] is ready to sacrifice herself with as much reason as heroism; [that she] is only in arms in consequence of her devotion to liberty and to the glory of all [– let France] cause this bloody conflict to cease!

It is for France to disarm Versailles by a solemn manifestation of her irresistible will.

Invited to profit by her conquests, she should declare herself identified with our efforts, she should be our ally in this contest which can only end by the triumph of the Communal idea or the ruin of Paris.

As for ourselves, citizens of Paris, our mission is to accomplish [the] modern Revolution, the greatest and most fruitful of all those which have illuminated history.

It is our duty to fight and conquer.

The only official programme of the Commune, 19 April 1871: *The Times*, 21 April 1871 (translated from *J.O.*, 20 April 1871). Passages in square brackets have been amended or added because they were left out or incorrectly translated in *The Times*; the declaration has been redivided into the paragraphs of the original French – the first two were omitted in *The Times*'s translation.

Citizen Members of the Commune,

You entrusted me provisionally with the post of War Delegate. I no longer feel able to accept this position of authority when the men under me do nothing but hold discussions and refuse to obey orders.

When it came to organizing the artillery, the Central Committee of the Artillery debated and made no rulings. After two months of deliberation the manning of your cannon is left entirely to the initiative of volunteers of whom there are too few.

When I took up my post at the Ministry I wanted to make it easier for us to collect all available arms, to requisition horses and to prosecute unco-operative citizens; to this effect I asked the Commune to increase the powers of the arrondissement municipalities.

The Commune debated the question and came to no decision.

Later, the Central Committee of the National Guard came to offer, almost imperiously, to participate in the war administration. The Committee of Public Safety having advised me to do so, I accepted this participation with no reservations, and I made the Committee a party to all the information I possessed on organizational matters. Since then the Central Committee has been debating but has not been able to act. In the meantime the enemy has mounted several daring and impudent attacks for which I would make them pay if I had the smallest military force at my command.

The garrison panicked, owing to incompetent leadership, and the officers held debates, expelled from the fort the dynamic Captain Dumont who had been sent to take command, and then, still debating, they evacuated their fort after foolishly suggesting to blow it up, which they would have been even more unable to do than they were of defending it.

The result of their confabulations: a plan, when what we needed was more men, a declaration of principles when what we needed was action.

My indignation brought them to their senses and they promised me for today, as a final and supreme effort, an organized force of 12,000 men, with whom I undertook to march against the enemy. These men were to have assembled at half-past eleven; it is now one o'clock and they are not yet ready. Instead of there being 12,000 they number approximately 7000, which is not the same at all.

Thus the ineptitude of the Artillery Committee has prevented the organization of the artillery, the hesitations of the Central Committee of the Federation have impeded administration, and the petty preoccupations of the officers of the Legion have paralysed the mobilization of troops.

I am not a man to hesitate in taking punitive measures; in fact while the Legion Officers were debating yesterday the firing squad was awaiting them in the yard. But I do not want to initiate tough measures and find myself

Louis-Nathaniel Rossel, the Commune's second War Delegate. A regular army officer whose disgust at the peace treaty with Prussia led him to join the Commune, Rossel resigned his post after nine days in protest at the Commune's military inefficiency.

alone in bearing the opprobrium of the executions that are necessary to turn this chaos into organization, obedience and victory. If I were at least protected by the people knowing about my efforts and my impotence, I would feel able to retain my mandate. But the Commune has not had the courage to make the situation known to the public. Twice already I have made the situation clear to you, but twice you have insisted on the matter being debated in a secret committee.

My predecessor made the mistake of trying to struggle with this absurd situation.

His example is a lesson to me. Since I am convinced that the strength of a revolutionary rests entirely on his refusal to compromise, I have the choice between two courses of action: to overcome the obstacle impeding my actions or to withdraw.

The obstacle cannot be overcome, for it is you and your weakness; I do not wish to offend against popular sovereignty.

I am therefore resigning and request a cell in Mazas [prison].

Rossel.

Letter of resignation from L.-N. Rossel, the Commune's second Delegate of War, 9 May 1871: Rossel, *Mémoires, procès et correspondance*, pp. 250–52.

Part Six: The Commune – The Debate on the Committee of Public Safety

The problem of organizing the military effort eventually led to a split in the Commune over the issue of forming a Committee of Public Safety. Everyone was agreed that a council of eighty could not act as an executive body, and so the debate (Document 19) centred on the name of the Executive Committee. A majority could not resist the suggestion, once it was made by the elderly Jacobin revolutionary Jules Miot, of taking up the name of Robespierre's Committee of Public Safety, which had organized the victory of the Revolutionary armies in 1793–94. The issue shows how hard it is to create new forms without looking back to the past; the strength of the revolutionary tradition in France was both an encouragement to revolution and yet was also a restrictive mould that had to be broken (see the public justifications of the voting, Document 20). The minority publicly withdrew from the Commune (Document 21), a move which only led to further dissension and accusations of treachery. The term 'Committee of Public Safety' was inextricably linked to the notion of terror and was repulsive to all moderate opinion; but the working population of the revolutionary districts welcomed the move and only demanded greater energy and more vigorous acts from the Commune (Document 22). Other members of the Commune received similar letters from the sans-culottes of 1871, and the popular clubs were likewise in favour of the new committee (see Document 27). The Paris branch of the International held a special meeting to debate the issue and came down, with some reservations, on the side of the majority (Document 23).

19 The debate

First session of 28 April

The following motion was tabled by Citizen J. Miot:

'Given the seriousness of the situation and the need for the most radical and energetic measures to be taken promptly,

'The Commune decrees:

'Article 1   A Committee of Public Safety will be formed immediately.

'Article 2   It will be composed of five members.

'Article 3   This Committee will be given extensive powers over the various Commissions and will be answerable only to the Commune.

J. Miot.'

Vaillant – Citizens, I have doubts whether you should vote today on a motion with such serious implications. Since all our members are not present, I feel that, however urgent the motion, the Assembly cannot make a ruling; it is not qualified to do so in the absence of the heads of departments. I think my views will be shared by many of my colleagues of the Assembly. Since they express all our various interests and tendencies, the different departments should be represented, and failing that, the Executive Commission should at least be present. We ought not to make a ruling on such a serious matter at the end of a session.

Régère – I do not think these demands are in any way excessive. When we voted on the Delescluze motion we were not acting as a government; a government must be united. The motion tabled just now is a move towards such unity. I therefore call for a vote of urgency. In my opinion the Commune will never succeed in guaranteeing public safety and defence unless it has a permanent and regularly constituted leadership composed of five members vested with the Commune's authority over the various ministers. I call for a vote of urgency. . . .

The question is voted a matter of urgency.

Régère – I move that the meeting be adjourned until tomorrow.

The Chairman – As your chairman it would seem to me that since we have taken a vote of urgency, discussion should follow immediately.

Rastoul – A week ago I took the floor to point out to you that we were heading towards the dictatorship that you were determined to avoid. Nine members were appointed.[1] I was opposed to this and requested that there be only three and at the most five. You could have called them a Dictatorship, a Committee of Public Safety, no matter; the point is that they would have had full powers. I therefore support the motion in favour of a Committee of Public Safety. My motion differs from Citizen Miot's in that I advocate that the dictatorship be in the hands of three members instead of five.

Billioray – I am in favour of a Committee of Public Safety. In fact the day after Delescluze tabled his motion I myself presented a similar proposal. We ought not to confer dictatorial powers on the War Administration, since this particular department is acting in total disregard of the Commune and ignoring its decisions. We are heading not only towards a one-man dictatorship but a dictatorship that will be ineffectual. If a dictatorship were a more effective means to victory I might agree to it (*cries of protest*). But the War Administration is the epitome of disorganization. We need a

---

[1] Along with the delegates to each of the Ministries, the Commune had at first formed a separate Executive Commission, which was abandoned in mid-April in favour of leaving the nine delegates to act in concert among themselves, as an Executive Commission.

committee with overall control over the activities of the various departments.

Babick – In my opinion the Commune ought to accept no other dictatorship than itself. The Executive Commission could well take offence at this motion; if some of its members are held to be incompetent, let them be replaced. I am against the dictatorship of a commission of three, five or nine members. Let the situation be saved by the Commune itself and not by a Committee of Public Safety.

Langevin – In my opinion we are bound too much by words. I have examined the Miot motion and I find it impracticable. With the Commune functioning as it does at present the activities of a Committee of Public Safety would be impeded. What have we been witnessing for the past week? The Assembly appoints commissions and then brings all the details of their work to us instead of referring back to the people it has appointed and discussing with them the way they carry out their work. When you have appointed an Executive Commission and called it Committee of Public Safety, the same thing will happen all over again (*Interruptions*).

Vaillant – . . . The proposal that has just been submitted is obviously a return to the previous structure with, however, extended powers being given to the new Commission's members. I think such an action would look very bad in the eyes of the public, to whom it would seem that we cannot make up our own minds. Remember, the new Commission was appointed barely six days ago. I really cannot believe that such grave events have occurred in the interim that we should need to change the present state of affairs. I would even venture to say that far from getting worse, the situation has in fact improved, and without necessarily giving the Commission credit for this it is nevertheless a fact I am pleased to record. If, on the other hand, there are accusations to be made, let us hear them and let the Commune, which is the supreme judge, decide. The Executive Commission, appointed six days ago, represents the aspirations of the Commune and up to now no complaints have been made against it; as the situation has improved since it was appointed I do not see any justification for abolishing it.

Vermorel – I agree with Citizen Miot that we must at all costs increase our control and our power to act. But at the same time we must not appear to change governments too often. There is, I believe, a way of reconciling the present motion with the existing state of affairs. What is happening now had been predicted; in fact I had suggested myself that the Executive Commission be considered as a sort of central commission of control which would not have to concern itself with details and paper-work, which are the business of the delegates. I think we can well retain the idea of a commission with overall control, composed, presumably, of five members;

88 it would not be called the Committee of Public Safety as that would

suggest an emergency situation, but the Commission of Control, of Investigation or some other more appropriate name. But beforehand I think it would only be proper to request that the Executive Commission present a report to you on its activities which would enable you to pass judgment on it (*Disturbance*). I believe in the need for greater unity of action and control, but I also think it is essential, for political reasons, not to appear in the eyes of our opponents or even of our friends to be abolishing today what we set up only a few days ago.

Babick – Citizen Vermorel has partly expressed my own thoughts. If there are any complaints against the Executive Commission, why not voice them immediately? Those who claim to have evidence that might justify an accusation are at fault for not making the facts known. For my part, I do not believe we are in danger. I have confidence in the principle of the Commune; it is above all treachery. I have faith in the Republic and in the destiny of the Nation regenerated by the Commune. This is why I cannot accept the creation of a Committee of Public Safety.

Vallès – Citizens, I think this whole debate revolves around a misunderstanding. It is the war that we are supposed to be discussing (*Uproar*).

Chalain – I do not agree that the public would disapprove of our going back on our decisions; on the contrary, I think it would congratulate us for going back on a wrong decision. It is our duty to change our plans when we have made a mistake. I do not think the Executive Commission should be dissolved but I do think it would be useful to have a committee that would hand down resolutions for the Executive Commission to follow (*Interruptions*). I am strongly in favour of a Committee of Public Safety. I believe it should be endowed with full powers which may even be used against members of the Commune; if it has proof of treachery on the part of one of them it should be able to break him (*More interruptions*).

E. Clément – I have only to repeat what you all know already. What is a Committee of Public Safety? It is a political commission. None of the members of the Executive Commission are in question here since this commission will continue in its present form. The delegates of the Commissions are specialized men involved in specialized tasks, who cannot be concerned with political questions.

Arnaud – This is obviously where the question lies. In my opinion the Executive Commission is not at stake. Each commission has special duties, but the duties of a Committee of Public Safety, unlike those of the other commissions, are entirely political. It is not a question of holding anyone in suspicion. Each commission is supposed to concern itself with a specific objective, while the objectives of a Committee for the Safety of the Public and the Revolution are quite different. I cannot therefore accept Citizen Vermorel's motion that this Committee be a controlling committee to whom the nine commissions would be answerable.

Amouroux – Citizen Vermorel gave me the impression of being afraid of the term 'Committee of Public Safety'. Let us have the courage of our opinions. Under the government of 4 September people were terrified of the word 'Commune'. Let us not be so frightened of words. . . .

Second session of 30 April

Johannard insists that the functions of the Committee be defined and its members be chosen among young and energetic men.

Allix points out that according to the conception of the Commune the new Executive Commission was in fact a Committee of Public Safety. He fears that they may be misled by the terms used: in this instance Committee of Public Safety is another name for dictatorship.

Chardon believes that the Committee can be set up without affecting the rights of the Commune.

Ostyn absolutely rejects the idea of a Committee of Public Safety: it is royalty in disguise. If it must be set up then its powers should be rigorously defined.

Vésinier thinks that the Committee of Public Safety would be in reality an Executive Committee over and above the existing commissions. It can be created without altering the present structure. Administrative duties take up all the time and energy of the members and delegates of the commissions; the role of the new Committee would be to lay down the political line. Can it constitute a threat? No, it cannot, if it is not backed by a Supreme Court with powers to arrest members of the Commune. If we do not set up such a legal body then the danger of a dictatorship will be averted and we shall achieve a two-fold aim: the Commune's inviolability will be assured and we shall have a strong leadership. . . .

Pillot believes that unity of purpose is necessary. Often – too often in fact – the Commune's decrees remain a dead letter. Among the general public certain groups have sprung up; they call themselves Republicans but their real intention is to destroy the Commune and replace it with some sort of Republic in the style of '48.

Vaillant thinks that they ought not to create a pastiche of revolution. The important thing is to change the nature of the Commune so that it becomes like the first Paris Commune,[1] an assembly of commissions working together, not a parliament where everyone tries to put in his word.

Tridon fears that the controlling committee would in fact be an obstruction committee. The enacting of decrees should not be the responsibility of a

[1] Of 1792–93.

single commission but of the entire Commune. Moreover he does not see which men should be selected to serve on this committee. . . .

Minutes of the debate in the Commune on the formation of a Committee of Public Safety, 28 and 30 April 1871 : *Procès-Verbaux de la Commune de 1871*, vol. i, pp. 556–62, 584–6, abridged.

Members explain their vote

1 I accept the binding nature of my mandate. I believe I am consistent with the promises and commitments I have made in voting for a Committee of Public Safety. *Th. Ferré* . . .

3 Considering that in the present state of emergency the term Public Safety has never been more appropriate, and that the Committee of Public Safety could never become a dangerous dictatorship, since it is under the control of the Commune, I vote in favour. *Parisel*

4 Given that the term Public Safety belongs to exactly the same era as the words French Republic and Paris Commune, I vote in favour. *Pyat*[1]

5 In conformity with the mandate received from my constituents, by which I am bound, I vote for the Committee of Public Safety because it is imperative that the Commune remain true to the broadest principles of the revolutionary movement that brought it to power. *Charles Gérardin*

6 I vote in favour of the Committee of Public Safety as an indispensable revolutionary measure in the present situation. *Ch. Ledroit*

7 Since I consider that the Commune cannot take too forceful a measure in the present circumstances, and since I wish to remain faithful to the mandate received from my constituents, I vote in favour. *Urbain* . . .

9 As we are being attacked mercilessly and without legitimate reasons I consider that we must defend the threatened Republic with all our energy. *Th. Régère*

10 I vote in favour, provided that the Commune may abolish the Committee of Public Safety whenever it wishes. *J. Allix*

11 I vote for the Committee of Public Safety because our situation is even more threatening than that of our forefathers of '93, and because those who attack the idea are not clear in their own minds. *Émile Oudet*

12 With the hope that the 1871 Committee of Public Safety will be what we generally but wrongly believed it to be in 1793, I vote in favour. *Raoul Rigault*

---

[1] Félix Pyat, like Delescluze and Miot, subscribed to Robespierre's Jacobinism and here justifies his vote in terms of the first French Revolution of 1789.

13 We consider that the setting up of a Committee of Public Safety will have the essential effect of creating a dictatorial power that will in no way contribute to the strength of the Commune;

That this institution will be in categorical opposition to the political aspirations of the mass of voters which the Commune represents;

That consequently the creation of a dictatorship by the Commune would be a veritable usurpation of the sovereign rights of the people;

We therefore vote against.

Andrieu, Langevin, Ostyn, Vermorel, E. Clément, Theisz, Seraillier, Avrial, Malon, Lefrançais, Courbet, Eugène Gérardin, Clémence, Art. Arnould, Beslay, Vallès, Jourde. . . .

22 Although I cannot see the usefulness of this Committee I do not wish to give cause for insinuations against my Revolutionary Socialist opinions. While I reserve the right to revolt against this Committee, I vote in favour. *Léo Frankel . . .*

27 I vote in favour of the decree but I do not share the illusions of the Assembly, which believes it has created a controlling political committee, a Committee of Public Safety, when it has merely revived under a new label the Executive Commission of our early days. If the Assembly wants a genuine Executive Committee truly able to take control of the situation and prepared for political emergencies, it should begin by reforming itself and cease to be a parliamentary talking-shop wantonly destroying what it created the day before and wilfully obstructing the decisions of its Executive Commission. The Commune ought simply to be composed of various commissions who meet to discuss the resolutions and reports prepared by each commission, who hear the political reports of their Executive Committee and judge whether this Committee is fulfilling its duty, whether it is able to provide us with a dynamic sense of direction and whether it has the energy and ability to serve the best interests of the Commune.

Political affairs would be referred to the Executive Committee and the various commissions would take charge of the affairs within their competence. No time would be wasted on unnecessary business and sessions would be spent in passing resolutions and not in speechifying.

I vote in favour without qualifications of an Executive Committee of this nature, which alone deserves the title of Public Safety (an unimportant title in any case, with the disadvantage of being redundant).

In a word, we must organize the Commune and its activities; we must have action and Revolution, not agitation and parody. *É. Vaillant*

28 For the same reasons as Andrieu and principally because I believe that a Committee of Public Safety would be ineffective – it is nothing but a word and the people have been put off with fine words for too long – I vote against. *A. Vermorel . . .*

32 I vote against because I dislike useless and ridiculous trappings which,

far from giving us strength, take away what little we have. *G. Tridon*[1] . . .

34 As someone who no more believes in words of salvation than in talismans and amulets, I vote against, for the reasons of order and justice put forth by Andrieu and also for reasons of common-sense and sound politics. *Ch. Longuet*

35 *Motion*:

I would like us to apply the titles and terms of the Revolution of '89 and '93 to that period only. They do not signify the same things today and are therefore no longer appropriate or meaningful.

The terms *Public Safety, Montagnards, Girondins, Jacobins* cannot be applied to a republican socialist movement.

What we represent is the period that has passed between '93 and '71, with our own genius corresponding to our own particular character.

It would seem to me all the more obvious that we are behaving like plagiarists and re-establishing to our detriment a terror that is out of keeping with our time. Let us use the terms suggested to us by our own Revolution. *G. Courbet*[2] . . .

Published justification for the way votes were cast on the issue of forming a Committee of Public Safety: *J.O.*, 4 and 5 May 1871; *P.V.C.*, vol. ii, pp. 33–37, abridged.

The minority declaration

DECLARATION

By a special and explicit vote the Paris Commune has surrendered its authority to a dictatorship which it has entitled *Committee of Public Safety*.

The majority of the Commune has voted itself no longer responsible and has handed over all responsibility in our present situation to this Committee.

The minority to which we belong takes the opposite view, namely that the Commune is beholden to the political and social revolutionary movement to accept full responsibility and not to delegate its powers to any other body, however worthy.

Like the majority we want social and political reforms, but unlike them we claim the right, on behalf of the voters we represent, to be fully

---

[1] Tridon was Blanqui's second-in-command, and his vote against the Committee of Public Safety shows that the division was not simply between Blanquists and Jacobins on one side and the more noticeably socialist members on the other.

[2] Courbet shows here signs of his earlier association with his friend P.-J. Proudhon, the French socialist and anarchist writer, who, for example, had written in 1848 that 'to create the new industrial forms of society does not call for the temperament of '93' (*Le Représentant du Peuple*, 29 August 1848).

answerable to those voters and not to shelter behind a supreme dictatorship that our mandate allows us neither to accept nor to recognize.

Therefore we will not sit on the Assembly except in cases where it shall constitute itself into a court of justice to try one of its members.

In a spirit of devotion to our great communal cause, for which so many citizens are dying every day, we shall withdraw to our arrondissements which we may have neglected too much of late. We are convinced, moreover, that the war takes precedence over all other questions at the moment, and whatever time we have to spare from our municipal duties will be spent among our brothers of the National Guard, participating in the decisive battle for people's rights.

Thus we shall serve our convictions just as usefully and avoid creating dissension within the Commune which we would all deplore, since we firmly believe that despite their political divergences majority and minority alike pursue the same objectives:

Political freedom,	Long live the Social Republic!
The emancipation of the workers.	Long live the Commune!

Declaration of the minority against the formation of a Committee of Public Safety, 15 May 1871, published in the Communard press on 16 and 17 May, 1871: *P.V.C.*, vol. ii, pp. 373–4.

22 A working man's letter

Citizen Babick,[1]

Citizen Miot's motion in the Paris Commune, relative to the setting up of a Committee of Public Safety, was much enjoyed by all the brave defenders of the Commune who are valiantly exposing themselves to the bullets of the Versailles tyrants.

But as for your protest it produced a very bad effect, and the citizens generously shedding their blood for the rights of Paris, for Justice and the honour of France are displeased and they are perfectly right.

Let us be brief and to the point. Is it true at present that the principle of monarchy can be established by the persuasion and free assent of public opinion? It cannot, you will agree. If the supporters of this principle were determined to make it prevail they would only succeed by tyrannical means, by coercion and violence – you would agree to this, would you not?

In the same way, can the republican principle be established in the present circumstances by persuasion and the free and voluntary assent of national opinion? I am sure you will answer that it cannot.

[1] For Babick's remarks during the debate on the formation of the Committee, see pp. 88 and 89, above.

If you are convinced of the truth of this, then remember that 31 October failed through the fault of two of your colleagues, Félix Pyat and Delescluze. Yes, these two citizens made it fail through their generosity, their loyalty and their honesty.

Let the Commune take care, or the same sentiments will bring about the destruction of everything we achieved on 18 March.

The hour has not yet come when our principle will triumph solely because it is right and because it recognizes the worth of man; society must first return to its normal state and it can only do so through the radical application of revolutionary measures.

Whoever at present opposes the carrying out of this objective will be held in suspicion, for he may contribute unwittingly to the downfall of the Republic and the victory of the monarchy.

If this misfortune should befall us the judgment of public opinion will be ruthless, for at present – let us not pretend otherwise – it is a question of life and death.

If any member of the Commune thinks he will escape punishment by the forces of reaction, he can be sure he will not escape punishment by the people. Therefore, dear Citizen, do not shrink from revolutionary measures; if your principles prevent you from carrying them out then at least do not obstruct them.

Working man's letter to Jules Babick, a member of the Commune, condemning the action of the Minority, 1 May 1871: A.H.G., Vᵉ Conseil, dossier 375; quoted in Rougerie, pp. 189–90.

Resolution by the Paris branch of the International

The Federal Council has passed the following resolutions:

Having heard the arguments of the Citizens of the International on the Commune and appreciating the perfect loyalty of their motives, the Federal Council calls upon them, while remaining dedicated to the workers' cause, to make every effort to safeguard the unity of the Commune so vital to our victory over the Versailles Government.

The Federal Council approves of their demand that the sessions of the Commune be made open to the public, and that Article Three of the decree establishing the Committee of Public Safety be modified, since it makes impossible all control over the actions of the Executive, that is, the Committee of Public Safety and the delegations.

Resolution passed by the Paris branch of the International concerning the action of the Minority: published in *J.O.*, 24 May 1871.

Part Seven: The Commune – Popular Sovereignty

Paris in revolution cannot be judged solely by the debates in the Communal assembly at the Hôtel de Ville. Popular opinion, the grass roots of the revolution, was better expressed in the papers that sprang up and in the clubs, which often established themselves in churches. A local section of the International wrote to the Commune urging it on in the cause of Justice and Labour (Document 24); ten days later in this same district the local club pronounced the dissolution of the Commune on the grounds that it was not sufficiently revolutionary. The clubs and the popular press restated the revolutionary political doctrine that sovereignty lay with the people, and that those elected as representatives could always be revoked (Documents 25 and 26). Here, incoherently and chaotically, can be seen the real violence of the revolution, and its energy. Issues debated covered matters of political sovereignty, spies, what to do with those who refused to fight for Paris. Typical of revolution in France was the virulent anti-clericalism. Class feeling was expressed in a mainly pre-industrial language, a hatred of the 'idle rich', who were seen as living off the sufferings of the poor (Documents 27, 28, 29 and 30). Clubs especially for women were also formed, as had occurred in earlier Paris revolutions; these in some cases paralleled the formation of a women's branch of the International, Élisabeth Dmitrieff's Women's Union for the Defence of Paris and for Aid to the Wounded. The three reports given here (Documents 31, 32 and 33) are all by men hostile to the Commune. Their bantering tone, addressed to a largely male readership, was intended to be at once disparaging and amusing.

24 Demand for greater war effort

We, delegates of the International, hereby deliver to you the present address passed by the General Meeting of the Montrouge section yesterday, Thursday, 11 May 1871.

Grave dangers threaten our social institutions. The members of the Commune have shown extreme sluggishness in producing not only the decrees but the revolutionary measures necessary to save the situation and ensure the success of the Revolution, which began so successfully on 18 March. Therefore the members of the above section appeal to you, their elected representatives, to remedy a state of affairs that will inevitably lead to our downfall if you persist in your present course of action.

Surrounded by devotional symbols and splendour, an orator addresses a meeting of the Club Communal in the Church of Saint-Nicolas-des-Champs. The anti-clericalism of the Commune represents a traditional element in French revolutionary thought, its origins stretching back as far as 1789.

In July 1849[1] a handful of workers held Cavaignac's forces in check for three weeks; they had neither cannons nor ammunition nor funds; the only weapons they possessed were some stones and a few old rifles. It is your duty to defend the same cause, the cause of Justice, the cause of Labour.

[1] The reference is to the June 1849 uprising, which was put down after three days of bloody street fighting.

97

You are masters of the citadel of Paris; you are a government at the head of a great power, the City of Paris! You have everything you need and more than enough weapons and men. If you were like the disinterested workers of '49 you could be twice victorious!

What must be done? We must spend as much as possible in times of war to defend the cause of justice, while economizing in times of peace. We must no longer procrastinate; our walls are collapsing under Royalist fire; cannons and machine guns are abandoned to the enemy from negligence or stupidity; the non-combatant units of the National Guard are bivouacking when they could be usefully employed building casemated and fortified barricades to neutralize enemy fire completely. . . .

What are you afraid of? You are masters of the situation; if you lack money you can always get more. Do you not realize that with each added day that your defence holds out another throne is shaken and more and more workers of the world, whose cause we are defending, come over to your side?

If you take these actions, if you are true to the principles of the institution you represent, then we, the International, will support you in every possible way, for our cause is the cause of Justice and we want it to be victorious.

Resolution sent to the Commune by the Montrouge
section of the Paris International, calling for greater vigour
in the war effort, 11 May 1871: A.H.G., Ly 22, abridged.

25 Editorial on popular sovereignty

Do not be too hasty to judge and take decisions in the name of the people and instead of them. Keep to your role of *mere attendants*. . . . You are servants of the people; do not pretend to be sovereigns, for the role befits you no more than it did the despots who came before you.

Your private persons are of little weight in the scales of the Commune. The people are tired of saviours; from now on they intend to question their actions.

Editorial (abridged) in the Communard paper *Le Prolétaire*,
19 May 1871, on the subject of popular sovereignty.
Le Prolétaire was published by the Club Saint-Ambroise in
the 11th arrondissement.

Contemporary sketch of a women's club meeting in a church in Montrouge. As in previous French revolutions, women broke from their traditional role to demand their political rights.

Declaration of principles by the Club Communal

The aims of the Club Communal are as follows:

To fight the enemies of our communal rights, our liberties and the Republic.

To defend the rights of the people, to educate them politically so that they may govern themselves.

To recall our mandatories to their principles if they should stray from them, and to support them in all their efforts to save the Republic.

Above all, however, to uphold the sovereignty of the people, who must never renounce their right to supervise the actions of their mandatories.

People, govern yourselves directly, through political meetings, through your press; bring pressure to bear on those who represent you – they cannot go too far in the revolutionary direction.

Should your mandatories hesitate or stall, spur them on towards the objective we all pursue: the conquest of our rights, the consolidation of the Republic and the triumph of Justice.

Long live the Commune!

Declaration of principles of the Club Communal of the
Church of Saint-Nicolas-des-Champs in the 3rd
arrondissement published in the first and only issue of its
paper, the *Bulletin Communal*, '*Organe des Clubs*',
6 May 1871.

The Chairman – I have received the following communication:

'The public meeting held on 1 May 1871, at the church of Saint-Nicolas-des-Champs, Rue Saint-Martin, at which about five thousand citizens were present, adopted the following resolutions:

'1 It requests that the Commune hold supplementary elections to fill the seats of those members who have resigned, as well as those who did not get a relative majority (half the votes plus one) at the last elections.[1] It asks the Commune to reply to this first resolution.

'2 The public meeting is *unanimous* in congratulating the Commune on its appointment of a *Committee of Public Safety*. It urges the Commune to persevere with energy and resolution in its revolutionary endeavour, which alone will be its salvation and will ensure the definitive victory of the Republic.'

This resolution was put to the vote and approved unanimously with great enthusiasm and repeated cries of 'Long Live the Commune!'

'3 The meeting at Saint-Nicolas-des-Champs also requests that the Commune make the churches of every arrondissement available in the evenings for public meetings and club sessions, to further the political education of citizens and keep them informed of the course of public affairs.'

The meeting asks the Commune to publish a statement to this effect in the *Journal Officiel*, instructing the delegates at each of the town halls of the twenty arrondissements to make places of worship available to the citizens of Paris for nightly public meetings.

It instructs Citizen Vésinier, member of the Commune present at the meeting, to convey its greetings to the Commune, and asks the Commune to implement these resolutions in the form of decrees and to inform it of any decisions taken.

The Chairman put the above resolutions to the vote, and the meeting, composed of at least five thousand citizens, adopted them unanimously.

1 May 1871

P. Vésinier,
Member of the Commune'

The Chairman – Could the Assembly now proceed to discuss this communication? *(Shouts of 'No!')*

Vésinier – I am not in favour of discussing this communication immediately.

---

[1] The reference here is to the April by-elections to the Commune, held to try to fill the places of those who resigned in opposition at the start of the Commune. In the by-elections there was a low turnout and several results were technically invalid because those elected had not obtained the legally required eighth of the registered voters. Two members did in fact resign. The club is here making its own interpretation in asking for a 'relative majority'.

I think it should be recorded in the minutes and receive attention in due course. I do not want to disrupt your agenda.

Resolutions placed before the Commune by Pierre Vésinier from the club in the Church of Saint-Nicolas-des-Champs at the session of 3 May 1871: *P.V.C.*, vol. ii, pp. 89–90.

Debate in the Club Ambroise

9 May

The Chairman opens the session at 8.20.

Citizen Jubelin takes the floor and demonstrates in clear and forceful terms the exceptional role played by Paris, the brain of France. His heart goes out to the citizenesses for their generosity and their virile energy in these times of great adversity. He mentions the dreadful threat looming over our intelligent people, the convict settlements of Lambessa and Cayenne that await us if we should fail. He ends by saying that rather than face the consequences of defeat he would die defending his legitimate rights (*Lengthy applause*).

In the absence of a speaker *Citizen Demar* kindly offers to address the meeting. An ardent follower of Paul Louis Courier,[1] he gives a clear-sighted analysis of the latter's democratic and social theories on the rights and duties of man, which are the ideas of the moment.

Giving his opinion as a man of experience he highly commends Renan's book on the life of Christ.[2] This work was condemned by the infamous Catholic Church whose errors and superstitions have had such a disastrous effect on the whole world.

He ends with a speech in favour of the principle of free and compulsory education, the foundation of universal literacy. . . .

Citizen Morel then takes the floor. He is concerned above all with the present critical situation. . . . He calls for the presence at each meeting of a delegate of the Commune to whom the club could communicate its decisions and who in return would inform the club of ideas produced in the Commune's sessions – in short, a direct link with the Commune.

The motion is put to the vote and carried unanimously. . . .

Citizen Beblin then goes up to the tribune, but he is repeatedly interrupted by noise and heckling and has to step down in favour of *Citizen Sallais*, a

---

[1] Courier (1772–1825) was one of the polemicists of the liberal opposition to the Restoration Monarchy.

[2] Ernest Renan's attack on accepted dogma in his *Life of Christ* (1863) led to his expulsion from the Collège de France.

young, unassuming man who in a few clear and forceful words addresses the meeting on the care of the wounded in hospital. He demands that the nuns, who no longer belong in the hospitals, be replaced by devoted citizen-esses.

The proposal to remove all nuns from service is put to the vote and unanimously approved.

Owing to a strongly worded intervention from *Citizen André*, an emergency vote is taken and carried, deploring the Commune's inefficiency in preventing certain regrettable events from occurring. . . .

Citizen Roussard then takes the floor to protest against the young dandies and others who are too cowardly to join the ranks of the National Guard and who even make fun of the principles it stands for. He calls for their incorporation into the National Guard. . . .

12 May

Citizen Missier points out that men are deserting from his battalion and that the gates are badly guarded. He noticed a guard questioning the orders he had been given. . . .

Citizen Parthenay discusses the subject of religion and concludes that we ought to get rid of all these religion-mongers.

Citizen Lesueur advocates that the churches be rented out, the proceeds to go to widows and orphans. . . .

Citizen Mativet says that up to now the Commune has more or less done its duty but it has made mistakes – for one, it is a pity that the Committee of Public Safety only has four members. . . .

Citizen Royer – There is not enough control over the activities of the Central Committee and the Commune.

13 May

Citizen Lesueur asks that his battalion be rehabilitated. Owing to a few deserters panicking everyone fled. He is not accusing the citizens of the battalion but the men who wear the stripes; he suggests that instead of staying in the rear the officers ought to head the battalion. . . .

Citizen Baillehache reads out a decree of the Commune: 'The Commune decrees a contribution of ten francs per day for fugitives.' The Citizen had heard about a man who had a considerable stock of potatoes and who would have liked to leave town but for the need to sell his potatoes first. Citizen Baillehache had the potatoes seized and sold for the benefit of widows and orphans.

Citizen Languetin asks that the Guillotine be brought back for all traitors as in '93. . . .

Citizeness Thyou . . . was passing by the Place de la Bourse[1] when she stopped

[1] The square in front of the Paris Stock Exchange.

a citizen to ask for some information. He replied that there were no 'citizens' in that neighbourhood, only ladies and gentlemen. The Citizeness asks that cannons be set up on the Place de la Bourse to silence all these reactionaries. On 4 May an artilleryman was arrested by a seminarist who made him kiss the cross while he was shot through with twenty bullets. . . .

14 May

Citizen Chardon calls for free and compulsory public education provided by lay teachers. The religious castes have prevented up to now the development of education among the working class, thereby depriving this class of its right to become free. The *coup d'état* of 1851[1] precipitated us into a state of ignorance where they would like us to stagnate forever. He attacks the politics of the men who are causing the bloodshed, meaning, of course, the Versailles Government. Education alone will save us by making every citizen conscious of his duty and his rights. . . .

Citizen Baillehache – A man named Caratain, a grocer of 39 Rue Servant, speculated during the siege, and by selling goods of poor quality made a profit of 70,000 francs. Since the proclamation of the Commune the said grocer has put a notice on his shop-front: 'Closed for restocking'. What is more, seven or eight shop-assistants of an age to bear arms have stayed behind in his shop. . . .

Citizen Rabaté . . . asks why the fort at Issy has not been blown up. He calls for determined resistance; not proclamations in the style of Favre, but action.[2] Blow up Paris rather than surrender.

Citizen Bouveron – Thiers ought to be eliminated at all costs; whoever does away with him will have deserved well of the country and the Republic.[3] He condemns the men who have prevented the emancipation of the people. . . .

Citizen Israel suggests that young clerks in commerce should be forced to bear arms. The offices of the Navy are full of youngsters with nothing better to do than smoke cigarettes.

A minor disturbance follows, after which *Citizen Baillehache* is able to make himself heard: . . . Let us take on the role of policemen and enter the houses and shops where the defaulters are hiding. Let us take them to 9 Place Voltaire where justice will be done to them. An insurrection was to be

---

[1] Which made Louis-Napoleon Emperor.

[2] The fall of the fort at Issy, a key position in Paris's defences, had brought about a crisis in the Commune; Rossel resigned and Miot suggested forming a Committee of Public Safety. Jules Favre, a republican lawyer, was Minister for Foreign Affairs in both the Government of National Defence during the siege and in Thiers's government at Versailles.

[3] Louis Michel, feminist revolutionary, went to Versailles immediately after 18 March with the notion of trying to assassinate Thiers; but she got no support from the National Guard Central Committee.

feared last night and may well occur tonight. The Municipality and the Committee have been and will be on duty night and day to weather the storm. . . .

16 May

Citizen Roullier asks whether or not it is feasible to set fire to the Bois de Boulogne. He dwells on the subject of the destruction of the Vendôme Column[1] and asks that a pedestal be erected in its place, bearing the following inscription: 'Twice Bonaparte ruled over France and thrice he delivered Paris to the foreign invader.' . . .

Citizen Sylvain asks that a deputation be sent to the Commune to call to account the members who intend to resign. He then inveighs against all defaulters and tables the following motion: 'That the shops of all refractory tradesmen be closed down, whatever their line of business.'

Citizen Baillehache interrupts the speaker to suggest he add to his motion that the goods be confiscated to provide for widows and orphans. The motion is put to the vote and unanimously passed. . . .

Citizen Baillehache asks . . . for the total suppression of all newspapers on the grounds that the reporters are not present during the fighting but get their information second-hand, hence the constant inaccuracy of newspaper reports.

Citizen Lemaître is most forceful in his reply, exclaiming that to suppress the newspapers is to put an end to freedom. . . .

Citizeness Thyou calls for the immediate arrest of all priests and their detention until the end of the war. She also asks that the Commune force landlords to exempt their tenants from the last three quarters' rent as well as rent for the month of July 1871.[2] . . .

Minutes of sessions of the club in the Church of
Saint-Ambroise in the 12th arrondissement, May 1871:
A.H.G., Ly 22 bis, abridged.

29 Meeting of the Club Saint-Michel

Citizen Moulin addressed the meeting on the subject of the barricades. Since the democratic worker-citizens are so few in number why do we not employ the aristocrats, the dandies, of whom there seem to be so many strutting up and down the boulevards with their pince-nez and their walking sticks, looking down their noses at the proletarian? . . .

Citizen Langevin wanted the Commune to be reminded that during the

---

[1] See pp. 146–49, below.

[2] See pp. 34 and 78, above, for the Commune's policy on rents.

first siege the Paris shopkeepers were making money in a corrupt way by selling their goods at exorbitant prices. They were sorry when supplies were brought in so soon as they would have been rich men today. These same shopkeepers are now leaving Paris and putting women in charge of their businesses. He requests that they be made to pay a fine of 100 francs per day for a week and that at the end of this period their goods be confiscated and sold for the benefit of the Commune and the widows and orphans.

All those present applauded this proposal and a delegation was appointed then and there to submit this justified demand to the Commune.

Report of a meeting of the club in the Church of
Saint-Michel in the 17th arrondissement, 14 May 1871:
A.H.G., Ly 22, abridged.

Meeting of the Club Saint-Leu

The first meeting took place on 6 May. It was chaired by Citizen Boilot who put the following motion on the agenda:

'Ought we to shoot the rich or merely make them give back what they have stolen from the people?'

One can easily imagine, given the audience of thieves and drunkards, what friendly discourse and conciliatory speeches such a discussion produced.

Citizeness Richon, a woman of the streets, was of the opinion that one should have no regard for 'the Croesuses of this world'. Another woman speaker advocated that all rich people have their incomes levelled to the sum of 500 francs. Finally, after prolonged discussion, the meeting decided that they should limit themselves to *making the rich cough up*, leaving it open whether to shoot them later. . . .

Report of a meeting of the club in the Church of
Saint-Leu, 6 May 1871: Fontoulieu, *Les Églises de Paris
sous la Commune*, p. 78, abridged.

Meeting of a women's club

The meeting began at eight with quite a good attendance and a very small minority of men. About two hundred women and girls were present; most of the latter were smoking cigarettes, and the reader will guess to what social class they belonged.

The Chairwoman, whose name we could not find out, was about twenty-five and still quite pretty; she wore a wide red belt to which two pistols were 105 attached. The other women on the committee also sported the inevitable red belt but with only one pistol.

A Polish woman by the name of Lodoiska was the official president but she had not wanted to chair the meeting as she intended to participate actively in the debate. . . .

The following point was on the agenda: 'How is society to be reformed?' Lodoiska spoke first but got a cool reception. A woman aged about thirty (now a refugee in Switzerland) was listened to with more attention:

'For people like us', she said, 'the social disease that must be cured first is exploitation by the employers, who are made rich by the labour of the workers. Let us do away with bosses who treat the worker as a producing machine! Let the workers form co-operative associations, let them organize their labour collectively and they will live happily.

Another evil of present-day society is the rich; all they do is drink and make merry without having to make any effort whatsoever. We must get rid of them along with the priests and the nuns. We will only be content when there are no more bosses, rich men or priests' (*Applause, laughter and murmurs*).

Next came a mattress-maker of the Rue Saint-Lazare who undertook to demonstrate that God did not exist and that the education of children should be reformed.

'What silly women we are to send our children to catechism classes! Why bother, since religion is a comedy staged by man and God does not exist? If he did he would not let me talk like this. Either that or he's a coward!' (*Murmurs from the crowd*).

The Chairwoman – Will the interrupters please be silent and let the citizeness speak.

The woman was thrown off course by the interruption and switched to a different subject, armed robbery and looting.

'There is something I would like to deal with briefly, the question of requisitions. I do not think these are conducted often enough. We have no linen or mattresses for our ambulances, while there is plenty of that sort of thing in rich people's houses. Our husbands and brothers who are defending Paris often have to go without while others have more than they can use. Everything must be evened out by searches and requisitions – it is the only way to achieve anything. A committee should be appointed in every neighbourhood to go out and search the houses in the name of the law, and we shall see what results we get. I know some people *what* have jewels enough to fill buckets.

A voice – But you're advocating theft! A disturbance follows with shouting and general confusion.

The Chairwoman – This is intolerable. I must have silence. If someone wants to refute the speaker's arguments let them step up here.

The mattress-maker left the rostrum, indicating by her gestures that the audience had not understood her.

Her place was taken by a little old woman who was always known in the neighbourhood as Mère Duchêne because of her ultra-revolutionary opinions and her irascible nature.

'My dear children', she said in a wavering voice, 'all this is so much hot air. What we need today is action. You have men – well then, make them follow the right track, get them to do their duty. What we must do is put our backs into it. We must strike mercilessly at those who are undermining the Commune. All men must be made to co-operate or be shot. Make a start and you will see! But no one wants to; they hesitate, they are afraid of a bit of blood. It makes me sad.

'If tomorrow we executed a hundred of those who are refusing to fight – which is not a lot – and exhibited their bodies on the boulevards with notices showing the crimes they committed, you can be sure that the day after tomorrow crowds of people would come forward to serve the Commune. What the Hell! The ends justify the means. But our leaders want to make omelettes without breaking any eggs and that cannot be done; on the contrary, you need to break lots of eggs. What are the lives of a few unworthy citizens when our future liberty is at stake? That's my opinion. We must frighten the reactionaries and the Versaillais by showing them that we are capable of punishing the guilty ones.' Applause breaks out but one or two derogatory whistles can be heard.

The Chairwoman (very irritated) – Would the Citizen Stewards please usher out the persons causing the disturbance. This is disgraceful!

The stewards looked round but could not spot any trouble-makers. Eventually the hubbub subsided and the debate was resumed.

A woman by the name of Nathalie Duval, wife of Lemel, was the next to speak. She was well known in the revolutionary party and in 1870 had founded, along with Varlin, an association called *The Soup Cauldron* which was apparently intended to provide the working class with cheap food but was in fact a secret society with entirely political aims.

Mrs Lemel did not make a long speech. She urged the women to take up arms in defence of the Commune and to fight to the last drop of their blood. 'The decisive moment is coming', she cried, 'when we must be prepared to die for our country. No more weakness, no more hesitation! To arms, all of you! Let every woman do her duty! We must stamp out the Versaillais!' (*Lengthy applause*).

Another woman went up to the rostrum, not to speak but to enact a grotesque parody of the rites of the Mass. This time the audience joined in with laughter, jeering and sarcastic comments:

'Hey, Mrs Guignol!'

'Look at the puppet show!'

'Down with the marionette!'

The Chairwoman in a rage gave orders to arrest the hecklers immediately, but they were so numerous that the stewards gave up trying to deal with them. So she closed the meeting, exclaiming that the neighbourhood was made up of nothing but monarchists, informers and Versaillais.

That was, in brief, the substance of the only meeting of the Club de la Trinité.

Report of a meeting in the women's club of the Trinité Church, 12 May 1871: Fontoulieu, pp. 271–75, abridged.

32 Speech made in a women's club

'Marriage, *citoyennes*, is the greatest error of ancient humanity. To be married is to be a slave. Will you be slaves?' – 'No, no!' cried all the female part of the audience, and the orator, a tall gaunt woman with a nose like the beak of a hawk, and a jaundice-coloured complexion, flattered by such universal applause, continued, 'Marriage, therefore, cannot be tolerated any longer in a free city. It ought to be considered a crime, and suppressed by the most severe measures. Nobody has the right to sell his liberty, and thereby to set a bad example to his fellow citizens. The matrimonial state is a perpetual crime against morality. Don't tell me that marriage may be tolerated, if you institute divorce. Divorce is only an expedient, and, if I may be allowed to use the word, an Orleanist expedient!' (*Thunders of applause*). 'Therefore, I propose to this assembly, that it should get the Paris Commune to modify the decree which assures pensions to the legitimate or illegitimate companions of the National Guards, killed in the defence of our municipal rights.[1] No half measures. We, the illegitimate companions, will no longer suffer the legitimate wives to usurp rights they no longer possess, and which they ought never to have had at all. Let the decree be modified. All for the free women, none for the slaves!'

Report of a meeting of a women's club in the Church of Saint-Eustache: Leighton, *Paris under the Commune*, pp. 282–83.

---

[1] On 10 April the Commune had adopted the widows and children of all National Guards killed in the civil war, and had specifically included in its decree women who were not officially married and their children; this recognized the situation, common in working-class Paris, of men and women living together with neither the blessing of the Church nor the sanction of the State.

The Times *describes a women's club*

Clubs, too, are cropping up on all sides – clubs for discussion of political affairs, clubs for disseminating inflammatory and irreligious sentiments, clubs for men and clubs for women. There have appeared in corners of several Red newspapers of late short notices that places of meeting would shortly be established where '*citoyennes* might congregate' and let off the steam of their enthusiasm. Two or three preliminary assemblies were held with closed doors at the *Mairie* of Passy, I suppose as rehearsals of a forth-coming performance. Within the last week, however, the plan has taken a tangible form; certain ladies make a circuit of the different Arrondisse-ments, laying down their articles of faith, and inviting all women to join in a common cause. . . . The meeting [we were to visit] was to be held on the Boulevard d'Italie, in the lowest quarter of Paris, some distance beyond Montrouge. After a drive of three-quarters of an hour we reached a kind of outhouse, surmounted by a red flag, and through the carefully-closed shutters of which came murmurs of subdued voices, and long streams of light spreading across the road. We entered the building without knocking, and found ourselves in a filthy room reeking with evil odours and crowded with women and children of every age. Most of them appeared to belong to the lowest order of society, and wore loose untidy jackets, with white frilled caps upon their heads. At the end of the room was a table littered with papers and books, and behind it sat a row of women, with red scarfs over their shoulders and red belts about their waists. None took much notice of us at first, being too much occupied with the oratory of a fine-looking young woman with streaming black hair and flashing eyes, who dilated upon the rights of women amid ejaculations, and shakings of the head, and approving pinches of snuff from the occupants of the benches near us. 'Men are *lâches*',[1] she cried; 'they call themselves the masters of creation, and are a set of dolts. They complain of being made to fight, and are always grumbling over their woes – let them go and join the craven band at Versailles, and we will defend the city ourselves. We have petroleum, and we have hatchets and strong hearts, and are as capable of bearing fatigue as they. We will man the barricades, and show them that we will be no longer trodden down by them. Such as still wish to fight may do so side by side with us. Women of Paris, to the front!' She sat down out of breath and rather confused, having had to bear up against considerable tittering on account of the imperfection of her French and the strangeness of her similes; but she looked very handsome, and might have sat for the portrait of one of the heroines of the first Revolution; but there was that in her eye which made me think as I looked at her that I should not like to be her husband. The next speaker seemed tolerably respectable, wearing a decent black gown

---

[1] 'Cowardly bastards'.

and bonnet, but her discourse was as rambling and inconsistent as that of her predecessor at the tribune. 'We are simple women', she began, 'but not made of weaker stuff than our grandmothers of '93. Let us not cause their shades to blush for us, but be up and doing, as they would be were they living now. We have duties to perform. If necessary we will fight with the best of them and defend the barricades, but I cannot think that so supreme a sacrifice will be demanded of us. We will attend on the battle-field and help to bring our wounded heroes back into the town, and thus save many lives which would otherwise be needlessly sacrificed. Yet another service we may render. We will establish portable cooking stoves, and cook the raw meat which is served out to the men of our army, which they throw away for lack of means to dress it.' Encouraged by the applause which had followed her thus far, she now degenerated into rant, attacking the priest-hood generally and the confessional, mimicking the actions used at mass amid the laughter and bravoes of the throng. One old lady became ecstatic, and continued digging me violently in the back with her elbow until the tears ran down her face and mixed with snuff that lay scattered over her countenance. 'Ah, the priests!' murmured another from under the heavy frills of her cap, a lady of a serious turn of mind, who nodded her head slowly from side to side as though it were a pendulum. 'Those priests! I have seen them too closely, *la canaille!*' This portion of the speech was the hit of the evening, and so the speaker kept up the subject for some time longer before launching into the history of Jeanne Hachette, and drawing a moral therefrom. She was listened to with respect to the end, great effect having evidently been produced upon her auditory by her immense command of historical detail. '*Elle s'y connaît, celle-là, ma chère*',[1] said one old woman to another with conviction, and an awe fell over the assembly, which permitted another woman, who looked like a laundress, to take her place behind the table. The new speaker was fluent and possessed a loud, shrill voice. She commenced a diatribe against all Governments as such, because, as she explained, they 'all caused the poor to sweat'. . . . The presence of the wretched male sex had already been remarked, sundry angry glances having been turned in our direction, and the newspaper woman, under the aegis of whose protection we had come, now suggested that it would be wise to retire, lest we should get hustled by an angry mob. We went accordingly, passing a lady in the doorway who held out a bag and solicited a trifle on behalf of the new society.

Report by the Paris correspondent of *The Times* of London of a women's meeting: *The Times*, 6 May 1871, abridged.

---

[1] 'She knows her stuff, that one does, my dear.' Jeanne Hachette, heroine of the siege of Beauvais in 1472, was famous for seizing a standard from a Burgundian soldier. An annual procession commemorated the event.

Three women await trial as pétroleuses. During the chaos of the last week of the Commune any working-class woman was likely to be arrested on a charge, almost certainly unfounded, of incendiarism.

Part Eight: The Commune – Social Measures (Education)

About half of those who sat on the Commune had been involved in the French labour movement, most of them having joined the International. Many (some thirty-five), though not all, were manual workers, or had been before becoming involved in labour politics. The Commune was regarded by both its opponents and supporters as implying social change – at least reform, if not necessarily revolution. The prime task of fighting a civil war did not prevent attempts being made to put into practice some of the most important demands that had been formulated within the labour movement as far back as the 1848 revolution and earlier. The two main fields were those of education and the organization of work. The Commune had taken over the Ministry of Education and had also set up a new body, the Commission of Labour and Exchange, to 'propagate social doctrines' and 'find ways of equalizing labour and the wage paid it'. The two delegates in charge of the Commissions of Education and of Labour and Exchange – Édouard Vaillant and Léo Frankel – were both committed socialists.

Education united republicans and socialists alike against the Church's dominance, re-established by Napoleon III, over the nation's schools. The programme of the New Education Society (Document 34) typically demanded a State-financed system of compulsory education, free of clerical influence, and one that balanced the traditional humanities with courses that would provide a useful technical training. Vaillant appointed a special commission (Document 35), which included two members of the New Education Society, to encourage local efforts, and a Jesuit school, with its well-equipped laboratories, was taken over and turned into the first technical or, as it was called, 'professional' school established by the Commune (Document 36). Women's education, even more the preserve of the Church, was another important field of innovation under the Commune. The initiative came from local organizations and teachers (Documents 37 and 39), and was backed up by the Communard press (Document 38). The language of Le Père Duchêne was deliberately modelled on that of Hébert's famous paper of the first Revolution, with its bougres and foutres, the swear-words avoided by polite society. Le Père Duchêne was also one of the several Communard papers that used the Revolutionary Calendar of 1793, which counted 22 September 1792 as the beginning of Year I.

Petition from the New Education Society

The delegates of the New Education Society were received yesterday by the members of the Commune, to whom they submitted the following petition:

To the Paris Commune

Considering the necessity, under a Republic, of preparing youth to govern itself by means of a republican education that has yet to be created;

That the question of education is a fundamental, all inclusive question that embraces and dominates all political and social questions, and that without its solution no serious or lasting reforms can be made;

That the institutions of education and training maintained by the Commune, the départements of the State should be open to the children of all members of the community, whatever their personal beliefs,

We, the undersigned, delegates of the New Education Society, urgently request, in the name of justice and freedom of thought:

That all teaching of religion and dogma be entirely left to the initiative and free choice of individual families, and that it should be immediately and radically abolished for both sexes in all schools and institutions maintained by taxation;

That these institutions of education and training should not allow in any place where it may be seen by the pupils or the public any object of worship or religious image;

That no prayers or dogma should be taught or practised in common in these institutions, nor anything that is of sole concern to the individual conscience;

That the method to be used exclusively is the experimental or scientific method, which is invariably based on the observation of facts, whatever their nature, be it physical, moral or intellectual;

That all questions relating to religion should be entirely excluded from all public examinations, particularly professional examinations;

Finally, that the teaching corporations should no longer exist except as private or independent institutions.

A good education is above all an education that is rational and complete, and proves to be the soundest preparation for life, whether private, professional, political or social. The New Education Society therefore expresses the additional wish that education be regarded as a public service of primary importance, and that consequently it be free and comprehensive for all children of both sexes, the sole condition being a competitive examination for vocational courses.

Finally it requests that education be made compulsory, in the sense that it become a right available to every child regardless of social position, and a duty for the child's parents or guardians, or for society. . . .

The delegates received the answer that the Commune was entirely favourable to a radical reform of education in the direction indicated, that it understood the capital importance of such a reform and that it considered their petition an encouragement to pursue a course of action to which it was totally committed.

Petition from the New Education Society concerning the
aims of education under the Commune, 20 April 1871:
J.O., 21 April 1871, abridged.

35 The Commission for the Organization of Education

Considering that it is necessary for elementary and technical education in the various arrondissements of Paris to be organized as soon as possible on a uniform basis;

Considering that it is imperative to hasten the change-over from religious to lay education wherever this has not yet taken place,

The Education Delegate of the Commune wishes to assist the Education Commission in these tasks by issuing the following decree:

1 A Commission is to be formed, entitled the Commission for the Organization of Education;

2 It is to be composed of Citizens André, Dacosta, Manier, Rama and Sanglier.

Paris, 28 April 1871.   Ed. Vaillant.

Decree appointing a special commission for the
Organization of Education to co-ordinate local activities
in this field, 28 April 1871: J.O., 29 April 1871.

36 Technical education

FRENCH REPUBLIC
LIBERTY EQUALITY FRATERNITY
PARIS COMMUNE

Technical Education

The first technical school is soon to be opened in a building previously occupied by the Jesuits at 18 Rue Lhomond in the 5th arrondissement.

Children aged twelve and over, regardless of the arrondissement in which they live, will be admitted in order to complete their elementary education
114 and at the same time to learn a trade.

Parents are therefore requested to register their children at the Panthéon Town Hall (5th arrondissement), stating the trade each child wishes to learn.

Workmen over the age of forty who wish to apply as instructors should also register at the above Town Hall, stating their trade.

We are equally appealing to teachers of modern languages, science, drawing and history who would like to co-operate in this new educational venture.

Paris, 6 May 1871.   The members of the Commission for the
Organization of Education, Eug. André, E. Dacosta,
J. Manier, Rama, É. Sanglier.
Approved by the Education Delegate, É. Vaillant.

Decree establishing the first technical school of the
Commune, 6 May 1871: *M.P.*, vol. ii, p. 438.

An industrial school for girls

Citizen Editor of the *Vengeur*,
I submitted the following proposal to the Hôtel de Ville yesterday, and hope you will see fit to print it.

*A proposal for the setting up of an industrial school
for training in women's occupations*

The aim of the industrial school is to revise and complete the scientific education of girls while affording at the same time sound vocational training.

To fulfil this aim groups of working women and groups of teachers or sufficiently educated women, more suited to intellectual than practical work, would be elected. The latter would undergo examination by a competent panel.

Together these groups would form the teaching staff of the industrial school.

The exchange of knowledge among women of different types of intelligence working side by side would provide a most favourable setting for a progressive education entirely free of prejudice.

The pupils would attend the industrial school from the age of twelve; practical work would alternate with the study of scientific theories and the industrial arts.

The State or the municipality, depending on their resources, would be able to assist the industrial schools, fix and guarantee their rent, pay the teachers and collect the manufactured goods from the workshop. As soon 115 as they are skilled enough to produce the pupils will be able to receive some remuneration.

The Industrial School would be a great improvement on the needlework school at present managed by nuns; it would be a truly professional school.

V. Manière,
Headmistress of the Provisional
Industrial School,
38 Rue Turenne.

Proposal for an industrial school for girls, 2 April 1871:
Le Vengeur, 3 April 1871.

38 Le Père Duchêne *on girls' education*

Père Duchêne or the grand gospel of women-citizens on what education should be given to the children of patriots to turn them into good buggers devoted to the Nation, and the grand baptism of Père Duchêne's daughter in the name of the Social Revolution!

He is the proud father of a daughter!

Yes, it's a true fact, Père Duchêne has become the father of a daughter and a healthy one at that, who will turn into a right strapping wench with ruddy cheeks and a twinkle in her eye!

He's as proud as a fucking peacock! And as he starts to write his rag today he calls on all good citizens to bring up their children properly, like Père Duchêne's daughter. It's not as if he's gone all toffee-nosed, but Père Duchêne is sure of one thing: the girl is going to get a bloody good education and God knows that's important!

If you only knew, citizens, how much the Revolution depends on women, then you'd really open your eyes to girls' education. And you wouldn't leave them like they've been up to now, in ignorance!

Fuck it! In a good Republic maybe we ought to be even more careful of girls' education than of boys'!

Because you know, patriots, that it's on a citizeness' knee that we stammer our first words, that we put together our first ideas and that we open the eyes of our mind as well as those of our body.

Right then! A good citizeness who is educated, who knows what it's all about and doesn't let herself be led up the garden path by the fucking priests – a true citizeness, in one word, is a good mother.

She keeps an eye on her nippers like a mother hen with her chicks. She takes good care of them and gets them to behave properly, and she would
116 have a fit if she saw them turn into bastards like Thiers, Favre, foul old

Picard, Vinoy – the dirty scoundrel – Gallifet and other scum of that sort! Good God, she'd rather hang herself, the poor woman, or jump in the fucking river!

There's nothing sadder for a good mother than to see her children go into fucking politics and get up to tricks they ought to be hanged for. Fucking Hell! No lie, it's bloody sad!

Christ! The cops of Versailles who are busy bombarding Paris and firing their bloody shells right the way up the Champs-Élysées – they must have had a hell of a bad upbringing! Their mothers can't have been Citizens, that's for sure!

As for Père Duchêne's daughter, she'll see to it her children are better brought up than that; when she's grown up Père Duchêne will have got lots of dough together selling his furnaces so he can let her have a bloody nice dowry and give her away to a good bugger, a worker and a patriot, before the citizens of the Commune!

Long live the Social Revolution!

Article from the popular paper, *Le Père Duchêne*, on girls'
education: *Le Père Duchêne*, 20 germinal, an 79
(19 April 1871).

Day nurseries

Education starts from the very first day of life; it is therefore important to decide how much and what kind of education is suited to the very young child, while recognizing, however, that the main aim at this stage of life is physical development.

If we accept the saying *mens sana in corpore sano*, then it is obvious that the development of the child's mind is affected by its state of health. A healthy mind cannot dwell in a sick body.

In present-day urban society, mothers pay nurses to look after their new-born children. The rich women do this often for reasons of vanity, the tradeswomen because the cost of months of wet-nursing is offset by their gainful employment, and the working-class women because it is impossible for them to do a heavy day's work and also provide the continuous care that an infant requires.

In the country children are usually raised by their mothers; the examination of the facts, that is, positive science, has established that this method of upbringing is the best and that we must return to natural practices. This confirms the principle that J.-J. Rousseau regarded as universal: that the so-called progress of civilization has brought about the degeneration of man.

Among all animals in the wild state the female suckles her young, and in these animals the degeneration of the races is unknown. Rickets have been produced experimentally by weaning animals prematurely, but they are never present in the natural state.

Given these facts, and since in an ideal society the product we must seek to perfect above all others is the child, it follows that the mother ought not to engage, during gestation and lactation, in any occupation that might be harmful to the health of her child or the quality of her milk.

To achieve this result economic reforms are necessary. Either the bread-winner's wages must suffice to maintain his family or the State must intervene, for our aim should be to arrest the process of physical and moral degeneration of the French people and to eliminate the consequences of involuntary poverty.

Until such a time as society is rebuilt on new political and social foundations, we must accept it as it is and apply such reforms as we can where the radical cure, in other words the Revolution, has yet to come about.

What are these reforms?

1 Up to now Public Assistance has paid an allowance to all unmarried mothers as an incentive to look after their children, and it has also given aid to needy women. But these payments were not sufficient to enable the mothers to nurse their children and thus build generations of sturdy youngsters.

2 Public Assistance has maintained institutions for children abandoned by their parents. These institutions are very costly to maintain; out of every hundred children admitted only three reach the age of twenty. These modern *oubliettes*, which will be regretted by no one except perhaps the staff whose livelihood they provide, should be closed down, and the capital they consume should be used for providing a substantial allowance for nursing mothers.

To those who fear that the payment of an allowance to unmarried mothers might be an incentive to promiscuity we can only reply that poverty and inadequate wages already have such dire effects that it is impossible for the result to be worse. In any case, if a mother nurses and brings up her child this is more likely to have a moralizing effect on her than if she abandons it to a poor-house. The latter solution leaves her free almost the day after the child's birth, without relieving her in any way from the poverty that will cause her inevitable relapse.

Until such time as mothers can be relieved of all outside work during nursing through the social reforms we advocate, the day nursery can be of considerable value to the mother and the child and therefore to society. It is a temporary remedy that preserves the family ties practically intact; it enables the child to be fed almost entirely by the mother, while she in turn 118 has time to engage in some form of work outside the home. However, the existing day nurseries must be modified to be genuinely beneficial to society. We consequently advocate the following changes:

1 Since the nursing of the infant by its mother, according to natural laws and scientific observation, is the only means of obtaining strong and healthy subjects, social reforms should be made to enable all mothers to breast-feed their children.

2 Day nurseries should be maintained on a temporary basis as the least defective means of promoting breast-feeding and fostering the natural bond between mother and child. The following reforms must be made in their organization:

The premises

These should be scattered throughout the working-class areas, near the large factories. They are to comprise four rooms and a garden. The neighbouring houses should be low, or else the nursery should be situated above street level so as to receive plenty of air and light; proper ventilation and cleanliness are essential.

Each nursery should provide for a hundred children, both toddlers and infants. There should be one room for infants, one for toddlers, a dining-room and a play-room. The premises should contain a kitchen.

In the infants' room the cots should stand one and a half feet apart and be draped with white curtains; they are to be made of iron and the mattresses of material that is easy to dry.

In the toddlers' room the cots are to be used for resting and the floor is to be covered with carpets on which the children may romp around.

The dining-room should contain a semi-circular table and benches of the right height for children. The inner area of the semi-circle allows for circulation while serving. Around the table there is to be a gallery with a double handrail on which the children may practise walking; this replaces the leading-strings and walking carts that deform the children's shoulders by lifting them too high. The children are to take their meals together, and, so that the wait between mouthfuls does not provoke screams, the entire staff should be present at mealtime.

The play-room is to contain everything to keep children amused; boredom is their greatest affliction. There should be a walking-ramp with double handrail around the table; all sorts of toys should be available, such as carts, an organ, an aviary full of birds; paintings or sculptures should be displayed, showing animals or trees, that is, real objects and not religious fabrications.

The garden is to be used as the season and the regulations permit.

Staffing and regulations

No minister or representative of a religion is to be accepted on the staff. 119

Each member of staff should be expected at any time to perform the most humble tasks.

A staff of ten is necessary for a hundred children: a matron, four women for the infants, three for the toddlers, one for the kitchen and one for the laundry. All these functions are to be rotated from week to week among those capable of undertaking them. The nurses in charge of the infants and toddlers should change duties every day, since the same daily routine would soon pall and make them dull and disgruntled. It is important that the children be looked after as far as possible by young and cheerful women. Dress should not be drab and black should be banished from the nursery.

The children are to be looked after during the night only in cases of absolute necessity.

The nursery regulations should be posted up in each room.

A physician and a chemist are to be designated by the civil authority on the recommendation of the staff of each nursery.

To prevent the spread of infectious diseases, children should not be admitted without examination by the doctor.

Proposal for the establishment of day nurseries for the
children of women workers: *J.O.*, 15 and 17 May 1871.

Opponents and supporters of the Commune recognized that it governed primarily in the interests of the working man. Opposite above, cartoon of the 'haves' and the 'have-nots'; while the financier slinks away from the Commune, the workman enters into a new prosperity. The placard beneath invites bakery-workers to a meeting to defend their newly won rights and to express their gratitude for the abolition of night-work, one of the few social reforms actually

Celui qui possède. Celui qui n'a rien.

LA COMMUNE 1871

LA COMMUNE 1871

Ça va mal!!. Ça va bien!!.

République Française

LIBERTÉ — EGALITÉ — FRATERNITÉ

AUX

OUVRIERS BOULANGERS

Quand on fait triompher la justice et le droit, manifester en masse sa satisfaction est un devoir. A cet effet tous les Ouvriers Boulangers, SANS EXCEPTION AUCUNE, sont invités à se réunir au Cirque national, le Lundi 15 Mai, à 4 heures du soir, afin de prendre une décision tres-sérieuse concernant les intérêts de la corporation, pour, de là, se rendre à l'Hôtel-de-Ville, exprimer notre gratitude à la Commune et l'assurer de notre dévoûment.

Pour la Corporation,

E. HENRY

Part Nine: The Commune – Social Measures (The Organization of Labour)

On 16 April the Commune decreed that trade unions might take over any factories which were closed down because their owners had left Paris for the safety of the provinces during the war against Prussia. The idea had already been mooted during the siege, both for patriotic reasons and in order to try to reduce the number of those without work. In its decree the Commune promised compensation to any owners who returned to Paris; some ten factories were taken over as a result of this decree. The idea that workers' co-operatives should replace capitalist production went back to the beginnings of the French labour movement, to the 'utopian' socialist theorists of the 1830s; during the 1848 revolution over three hundred meetings on this subject had been held in different factories. The co-operative idea was very common in the French section of the International (Document 40). The strong anti-State element of French socialism, seen for example in P.-J. Proudhon's writings and in the close links between anarchism and workers' organizations, meant that the aim was not nationalization – State control over areas of the economy – but the formation of independent producers' co-operatives. The State, especially since in Paris this now meant the Commune, was looked to for aid in starting up such co-operatives (Documents 41, 42 and 43). At a time of economic crisis and war, such as 1871, the particular areas where the Commune was expected to act were armaments (Document 44), as had happened under the Jacobins in 1793, and the provision of clothing for the National Guard (Document 45). At Frankel's initiative a special report was prepared on the bulk purchasing of National Guard uniforms (Document 46). As this was largely women's work the Women's Union for the Defence of Paris, under Élisabeth Dmitrieff (Document 47), petitioned the Commune for an increase in wages paid for the production of uniforms and, more generally, for the equalization of conditions between male and female workers (Document 48). Frankel and his Commission ensured that the Commune did not go back on its promise to regulate the conditions of work in the bakeries by abolishing night-work. The bakery workers had been pressing for this for years. The proprietors strongly opposed the measure, and the debate in the Commune (Document 49) shows that not all members were willing to transgress orthodox liberal economic principles such as the 'freedom of contract' between a worker and his employer.

A stone-carver's letter

Allow me to suggest what seems to me the most logical and practical way of dealing with our present society, which is organized on entirely different principles from those we are seeking to apply.

My aim in submitting the following proposal to the International is to stimulate its activities and encourage its Paris supporters to form themselves into co-operatives which would establish branches in each section and if necessary in each arrondissement.

Each co-operative should choose leaders among their ablest members, and these leaders should organize, with the financial aid of the whole International, a co-operative manufactory to undertake all work available in the City of Paris at the most advantageous prices possible.

If there is competition from private enterprise the prices should be fixed at a level such that the employers will not be able to survive unless they exploit their workers mercilessly. In this event the workers would be forced to join our ranks out of personal interest, and in doing so they would be able to organize a most effective strike.

To achieve these ends the International, our universal mother, should set up in Paris, either with its own funds or by means of a contribution from all its members, one or two co-operatives with essential functions and a large membership. Once established the co-operatives would take charge of all the work immediately available. Functioning and producing profitably, they would easily be able to set aside 10 or 15 per cent of the proceeds of their work towards the setting up of other co-operatives. This sum would be used to pay off the loan from the contributions.

The running of the first co-operative would obviously serve as a model and an aid for the eventual organization of all the trades on a co-operative basis. When we have thus abolished all exploitation by private employers and have gained control over our own production we will easily force Commerce and Capital to bend to our laws.

All the co-operatives in other countries would follow the same procedure, again with the aid of the International, until the system of co-operative associations will become universal.

When we have thus succeeded in obtaining control over our own production, when the International has attracted the ablest workers from every industry, it will then be able to set up vast national stores where the goods produced by all co-operative members will be sold on behalf of the co-operatives at a profit of only 10 or 15 per cent. These stores would be run by men or women citizens of the International, and the various goods and products would be sold only to members for their personal consumption.

The products supplied by the International to the consumer would still be on average almost 35 per cent cheaper than the goods produced by the employers and handled by the tradesmen, because of the enormous profits these agencies are obliged to deduct. . . .

Several advantages would result from this system. The first is that it would not conflict in any way with the selfish and absurd social laws that govern us. The second is that it would provide regular employment for all the workers of the co-operatives, and the regularity of this work would amply compensate for the 10 per cent the co-operatives would have to part with for the establishment of other co-operatives; the third advantage is the inevitable abolition of the class of employers and of the exploitation of man by man.

Letter from a stone-carver (*ouvrier sculpteur*) to the
Commission of Labour and Exchange: A.H.G., Ly 11,
abridged.

41 *The organization of women's work*

The Revolution of 18 March was spontaneously accomplished by the people in circumstances unique in history. It is a major victory for the rights of the people in their relentless battle against tyranny, a battle that was first waged by the slave, was continued by the serf and will be gloriously brought to an end by the proletarian through the Revolution of social equality.

The new movement was so unexpected and so radical that it was beyond the understanding of professional politicians, who merely saw it as an insignificant, aimless revolt.

Others have tried to belittle the spirit of the Revolution by reducing it to a mere demand for 'municipal rights', for some kind of administrative autonomy.

But the people are not taken in by the illusions perpetrated by governments, nor by so-called parliamentary representation; in proclaiming the Commune they are not demanding certain municipal prerogatives but communal autonomy in its greatest sense.

To the people the Commune does not merely signify administrative autonomy; above all it represents a sovereign authority, a legislative authority. It stands for the entire and absolute right of the community to create its own laws and political structure as a means to achieving the aims of the Revolution. These aims are the emancipation of labour, the end of monopolies and privileges, the abolition of the bureaucracy and of the feudalism of industrialists, speculators and capitalists, and finally the creation of an economic order in which the reconciliation of interests and a fair system of exchange will replace the conflicts and disorders begotten

by the old social order of inaction and *laissez-faire*.

For the people the Commune is the new order of equality, solidarity and liberty, the crowning of the communal Revolution that Paris is proud to have initiated. . . .

Today it is the duty of the Commune to the workers who created it to take all necessary steps to achieve constructive results. . . . Action must be taken and it must be taken fast. However, we must not resort to expedients or makeshift solutions that may sometimes be appropriate in abnormal situations but which only create formidable problems in the long run, such as those resulting from the closure of the National Workshops in 1848.[1] . . . The Commune must abandon the mistaken ideas of old, it must gather inspiration from the very difficulties of the situation and apply methods that will survive the circumstances that first led to their use.

We will achieve this through the creation of special workshops for women and trading centres where finished products may be sold.

Each arrondissement would open premises where the raw materials would be taken in and distributed to individual women workers or to groups according to their skills. Other buildings would receive the finished products for their sale and storage.

The necessary organization for the application of this scheme would be under the control of a committee of women appointed in each municipal district.

The Commune's Commission of Labour and Exchange could organize the distribution of raw materials to the arrondissements from a vast central building.

Finally the Finance Delegate would make a weekly credit available to the municipalities so that work for women can be organized immediately. . . .

Proposal for the organization of women's work from a
printer member of the Commission of Labour and
Exchange: A.H.G., Ly 23, abridged.

2 A nail-maker's letter

Paris, 26 April 1871

Citizens,

The Commune is placing orders for nails with the bosses; this is not right. It should address itself to the workers first. I am a National Guard, a

---

[1] In the first enthusiasm after the February 1848 revolution the government established, under the socialist writer Louis Blanc (who stayed safely at Versailles during the Commune), a Workers' Commission which set up the National Workshops as a State employment system. It was the closure of these workshops that sparked off the June 1848 workers' uprising.

Communist and a long-time member of the Trade Union, and I am not working because I refuse to work under the Commune for a boss – one is too much of a slave.

Send me five requisition orders to make 100 kg. of nails and five orders for 50 kg. of coal. When the nail-makers will see that they will come running to join the workers' federation.

Citizens, honour my request, not for me but for my fellow-workers. They are all for the Commune but they do not understand it. However, I do all I can to promote unity; it is up to you to help me by granting my request.

With fraternal greetings,

Roulleau, 76 Rue Dasnier, Paris.

Letter to the Commune from a nail-maker demanding
direct trade between the Commune and workmen, Paris,
26 April 1871: A.H.G., Ly 23 (orthography corrected).

43 A railway-worker's letter

2 May 1871

Citizen Père Duchêne,

I have just read an article in your issue of yesterday about doing away with bakers' night-work[1] and I'm bloody pleased for them.

But I want you to know a bit about the railway services. I am one of the older workers, of twenty years employment on the Orleans railways, having sacrificed my youth working nights and days of eighteen to twenty hours out of twenty-four, and all the time earning only 1 fr. 50 a day which is 45 fr. a month. . . . How is one to feed a family?

We are on a fortnight's day-shift and a fortnight's night-shift, from half past four in the afternoon until seven or eight in the morning. Unloading the trains, heaving the goods about all the time with no break. They drive us like galley-slaves; the slightest little mistake and it's a two to five franc fine and you haven't the faintest idea what you've done wrong. I can tell you it's bloody hard. . . .

They are crooks, these railway bosses, there's no doubt about it; they easily make 100,000 francs in gratuities while their wretched subordinates work to fill their fat bellies. . . .

We kept watch in the stations all winter to guard their buildings and trains; they kept promising us we would be armed but until the end we never were. We did various duties for the market porters, the ambulance-men, the bakers, but we were not given any of the outside support the National Guard had, such as a bread allowance and the 75 centimes for

¹ See Document 49, pp. 136–39, below.

wives. We got no supplement to our pay. We would very much like to know whether we will be able to have clothing like the other citizens who have not been armed. It is not our fault if they wouldn't give us arms; we asked for them often enough. Imagine, they are making us pay the National Guard's clothing expenses by making a deduction from our wages! We ask Citizen *Père Duchêne* to give it to them straight, until such time as we can bring these matters to the attention of the Commune, which seems to be too busy right now with the narks of Versailles.

Citizen A. Rossen, railwayman.

Letter to *Le Père Duchêne* from a railway-worker,
2 May 1871: Adamov, *Anthologie de la Commune*,
pp. 115–16; *Lettres au 'Père Duchêne' pendant la Commune
de Paris*, pp. 59–61, abridged.

◀ ## Regulations of a factory co-operative

Workshop at the Louvre for the repair and conversion of arms
Regulations submitted for approval to the Paris Commune by the workers of the Louvre workshop.

Article 1 The workshop is to be managed by the delegate to the Commune. The manager will be elected by all the workers and will be liable to be revoked if found guilty of failing in his duty. His mandate consists in hearing the reports of the shop foreman, the charge-hand and the workers, and in submitting them to the Director of Artillery Supplies. He will give a precise account of his dealings both in and outside the workshop to the Council (see below).

Article 2 The shop-foreman and the charge-hand will also be elected by all the workers. They will be accountable for their actions and will be revocable in the same way as the Commune delegate if it can be shown that they have failed in their duty.

Article 3 The duties of the shop-foreman are to supervise the workshop, to hand out and collect the work, to check the arms and to keep an account of the hours put in by the workers, based on the check kept by the charge-hand. All workers are to clock in within a quarter of an hour after the opening of the workshop.

Article 4 The duties of the charge-hand are to hand out and supervise the work on their respective lathes. They must give the workers all the necessary information for the carrying out of their tasks. They must report in detail every day on all work carried out under their supervision.

Article 5 The checking of the arms on entry and exit will be carried out by specialized workers who must be able to assess the condition of the arms. 127

They will be elected by the workers and will also be subject to dismissal by the workers at the suggestion of the Council. Both checkers will be assisted by a clerk appointed by the Council.

The Council

Article 6 There will be a Council meeting every day without fail, after the shift ending at 5.30 p.m., to discuss the next day's work and the reports and suggestions submitted by the manager, the shop-foreman, the charge-hand or the worker delegates, of which mention will be made later.

Article 7 The Council will be composed of the manager, the shop-foreman, the charge-hand and one elected worker from each workbench.

All members of the Council are duty-bound to attend; the manager alone, because his function is essential, may be excused from attending in an emergency; he will then inform the Council of the reasons for his absence.

Article 8 The delegates will be completely replaced every fortnight; half of them will be replaced every week.

Article 9 The delegates will inform the workers of what is said at the meetings; they will act as their spokesmen on the Management Council and put their suggestions and grievances before the Council.

Article 10 The majority of the delegates is always entitled, at the request of one of the delegates, to call a meeting of the Council. In the case of a refusal on the part of the charge-hands, the shop-foreman or the manager this majority has the right to refer the matter to the workers as a whole.

Article 11 To safeguard the interests of the Commune, the delegates will form a control committee and will have the right to ask for information on all dealings within and without the workshop. They may ask to see the books whenever they judge necessary.

Article 12 At the beginning of every week the delegates will elect a secretary whose duty it will be to report on everything of importance that is said and done in the course of a week. These reports will be posted up outside the workshop, in an obvious position, for the whole of the following week. They will then be collected but remain available for reference.

Article 13 Workers will be taken on as follows: on the recommendation of the shop-foreman the Council will decide whether workers will be taken on and in what number. Potential workers may be recommended by any worker or employee of the workshop. Their names will be entered in a special book and they will be taken on in order of entry. The Council will decide what tasks they are capable of.

Article 14 Workers may only be dismissed by a decision of the Council, after hearing the shop-foreman's report. If there is a reduction in work the workers taken on last will be dismissed first, unless one or more older workers are judged by the shop-foreman to be guilty of extreme inefficiency

The long gallery of the Louvre, converted into an armaments workshop during the war against Prussia. Under the Commune the workers took over and administered the factory as a co-operative.

or misconduct, in which case the Council alone is empowered to make a decision on their future.

Article 15 The working day will be 10 hours; the workshop will be open from 7 a.m. to 6 p.m., with a lunch-break from 11 to noon.

In exceptional cases, where a repair order has to be carried out immediately in the interest of the Commune's defence, the Council will decide whether it is necessary to work one or more hours' overtime. However, this overtime, which must only be worked in exceptional cases, will be paid at the normal rates already fixed for each worker. . . .

Article 17 The salary of the manager is fixed at 250 fr. a month, with no additional interest or bonus.

Article 18 The salary of the shop-foreman is fixed at 210 fr. a month. He is bound to be present when overtime is necessary, but can claim no extra pay. 129

Article 19 The wages of the charge-hands will be paid daily at a rate of 70 centimes an hour.

Article 20 The workers' daily wage will be fixed by the Council on the recommendation of the charge-hands; however, given that we are at war, it cannot go beyond 60 centimes an hour.

Article 21 If a supervisor, for one reason or another, takes up the duties of an ordinary worker his new daily wage will be fixed by the Council.

Article 22 The present regulations may be modified with the agreement of the Director of Artillery Supplies, on the suggestion of the Council and the absolute majority of the workers.

Drafted in duplicate at the Louvre, 3 May 1871.

Regulations of the Louvre armaments factory co-operative,
3 May 1871: *J.O.*, 21 May 1871, abridged.

45 Letter from the tailors' co-operative

We, the undersigned citizens, who have always considered the Revolution of 1871 to be based on the emancipation of the Proletariat, find ourselves regretfully obliged to stop work due to the reaction of Capital.

We wish to inform you that Citizen Leborgne, in the name of a co-operative association of tailoring workers, obtained from Colonel Fabre an order for two thousand garments, both tunics and trousers.

The Citizen Delegate for Military Supplies withdrew the order under the pretext that capitalist manufacturers could supply the goods at a lower price. How are they able to do that? We would never wish to be associated with such a scheme; it can only be carried out by lowering the payment for labour. The aims professed by the Citizen in charge of placing these orders will not be fulfilled at all, since Capital will retain the same profit and merely lower wages as the market prices are lowered.

Things would be quite different if the workers' co-operative associations were protected by those in favour of the emancipation of the Proletariat and the consolidation of the Great Revolution that has just taken place.

Letter to the Commune from the tailors' co-operative:
A.H.G., Ly 22.

46 The supply of military uniforms

Our investigation of contracts concluded up to 25 April 1871 shows that military uniforms were being purchased from the manufacturer by the City of Paris at 6 francs per tunic and 3 fr. 50 per pair of trousers. This remuneration was enough to support the men and women thus employed.

After this date, however, certain manufacturers have put in tenders of 4 francs or even 3 fr. 75 per tunic and 2 fr. 50 per pair of trousers. These tenders are now going through. The result is that the payment for labour, which was already very low, is now being cut almost by half and the tailoring workers will not be able to survive. Thus the Revolution has brought about the following situation:

The work contracted by the Commune for the National Guard will be paid much less than under the Government of 4 September, and the Social Republic can now be accused of an action the Versaillais were not guilty of: it has lowered wages.

It ought to be made clear whether the Commune wants to help people to live on charity or by their own work. We are told that the government is obliged to count the pennies, 'to conclude deals at the lowest possible price'.

We wish to emphasize that this is not a commercial matter nor a special case but a question involving the totality of the labouring population. If the seamstress, instead of earning two francs per day, only earns one franc, she will obviously have to resort to soup-kitchens and to Public Assistance, which will not only cost the Commune just as much but will have a detrimental effect on morality.

It is with great reluctance that we submit a report showing such lack of harmony between the policies of the Government and its socialist principles. We are distressed to observe that the manufacturers, in spite of offering such low prices, are still in a privileged position.

The workers' co-operative associations cannot agree to take part in exploiting the destitution of the people in order to lower manufacturing costs. If the Commune wishes to have supplies of good quality and good workmanship it ought to address itself directly to the workers of the Tailors' Association of Paris. We maintain that it is impossible to produce clothing in proper conditions given the prices agreed on by the latest signatories to the supply contracts.

We wish to warn the Commune against a policy that threatens the highest principles of the Social Revolution. We must aim constantly to protect the Social Revolution from such dishonour and not let petty speculations undermine the grandeur and prestige of our movement.

The Citizen Delegate for Public Works must at all costs persuade the Commune not to be impressed by the low prices offered by the manufacturers.

We recognize that the workers' co-operative associations cannot at present compete with private enterprise; they will never be able to do so without material and moral support.

Production costs will only be lowered when the co-operative associations are their own masters.

We conclude by demanding that the piece-rates for National Guard uniforms remain as they have been for the last eight months, and that all contracting and manufacture of clothing be as far as possible handed over to the Tailors' Association.

All three organizations, the Tailors' Co-operative Association, the Federation of Trades Unions [Chambre Syndicale] and the Workers' Mutual Aid Society [Société de Résistance], representing the workers in the tailoring trade, have just handed to us a contract (on a federal basis), placing at our disposal the 20,000 or 30,000 workers of the trade.

The following is the Commission's report:

Report on the Inquiry into Negotiations for Military Uniforms

According to the terms of the Commune's decree of 4 May 1871, the Commission of Labour and Exchange formed a Committee of Inquiry to report on the contracts concluded by the Commune for the supply of military uniforms.

The report of the Committee reveals that since 18 March, the Administration, beguiled by the offers of the manufacturers, has lowered the piece-rates for uniforms to a considerable degree.

At first sight this policy seems perfectly reasonable: the Commune was looking for firms with which to do business and concluded deals with those offering the most advantageous prices.

Under this system the costs of manufacture will most certainly drop still further. The businessmen concluding such deals run no risks at all; they make up their losses by paying lower wages – why should they mind putting in tenders at bargain rates? The men and women in the tailoring trade, driven by a shortage of work, will always be prepared to bear the whole brunt of the lowering of prices. . . .

As for the manufacturers, they reap all the benefits and they run no risk of losses; between the price agreed on with the Commune and the wages they pay there is always a margin with which to fill their pockets. . . .

It all boils down to this: the manufacturers are taking advantage of the people's destitution to lower wages, and the Commune is blind enough to condone these machinations.

To have recourse to an intermediary whose sole function is to deduct a commission on the wages of the workers he employs is both useless and immoral. The worker continues to be enslaved by the employer, who holds absolute control over production. It is a perpetuation of the slave-driving traditions of bourgeois régimes whose self-interest makes them the inveterate enemies of working-class emancipation.

It is not valid to invoke the state of our finances; as the Committee's report rightly points out, *if a family cannot support themselves by their own*

work they will have recourse to Public Assistance, which will result in a burden on public funds. It is an irrefutable economic fact that the worker will claim from charity what his work cannot provide; the only one who benefits is the employer, as we demonstrated earlier. . . .

Meanwhile, the worker is getting killed on the ramparts to put an end to this very kind of exploitation!

Conclusions

The Commission of Labour and Exchange requests that the workers' associations be awarded all contracts that may be negotiated directly with them.

Prices will be agreed upon by the Department of Military Supplies, the Tailors' Trade Union and the delegates from the Commission of Labour and Exchange.[1]

The Commune's Delegate on the Commission of Labour and Exchange,
Léo Frankel.

Frankel – I would just like to add a few words to this. We must not forget that the Revolution of 18 March was accomplished solely by the working class. If we do nothing to assist this class, we who believe in social equality, I can see no reason for the Commune's existence.

Malon – I agree with Citizen Frankel and I would add that various secretaries of workers' co-operative associations have come to ask me whether it would be possible to cancel the existing contracts. . . .

Report to the Citizen Delegate for Public Works on
contracts for the supply of military uniforms, 12 May 1871:
P.V.C., vol. ii, pp. 348–56, abridged.

7 Letter from Élisabeth Dmitrieff

24 April 1871

Dear Mr Jung,[2]

It is impossible to send letters by the post since communications are severed and everything falls into the hands of the Versaillais. Seraillier, who has just been elected to the Commune and who is in good health, sent seven

---

[1] In the event the Commune did not go quite as far as its Commission recommended; existing contracts were to be revised and future ones to include a stated minimum wage rate, with preference given to workers' co-operatives.

[2] Jung was a Swiss watchmaker who lived in London and was a member of the London General Council of the International. On Élisabeth Dmitrieff, see glossary of names, p. 171, below.

Élisabeth Dmitrieff, founder of the Women's Union for the Defence of Paris and for Aid to the Wounded. The Union, in effect a women's branch of the First International, actively defended the interests of female garment workers.

letters to Saint-Denis which reached that destination but apparently were not received in London. I had sent you a telegram from Calais and a letter from Paris, but since then, although I have searched everywhere and tried to inform myself, I can find no one who is going to London.

How can you possibly stay there doing nothing when Paris is about to perish because of people like you? We must at all costs stir up the provinces to come to our aid. The people of Paris are fighting heroically (some of them, that is), but we never expected to be abandoned in this way. However, up to now we have maintained all our positions, Dombrowski[1] is fighting well and Paris is truly revolutionary. Supplies are not lacking. I am a pessimist, you know; I have no illusions and I expect to die one of these days on a barricade. We are expecting a general attack. . . .

I am very sick with bronchitis and a fever. I work hard; we are mobilizing all the women of Paris. I organize public meetings; we have set up defence committees in all the arrondissements, right in the town halls, and a Central Committee as well, all in order to organize the Women's Union for the Defence of Paris and for Aid to the Wounded. We are getting in touch with the Government and I think the project will succeed. . . . If the Commune is victorious our organization from being political will become social, and we will form branches in other countries. . . . We did not get the Manifesto to the farm-workers out soon enough. I do not think it was written at all and this in spite of all our warnings. The Central Committee had not given up its powers immediately and difficulties arose that weakened

---

[1] Dombrowski, a Polish aristocrat and officer who escaped to Paris from Russia, after rescuing his wife from Siberia, was the best of the Commune's commanders in the field; he died in the fighting during the final week.

the various parties. But since then everything is being organized on a firmer basis. I think we have done what we could.

I cannot say too much, for fear that Monsieur Thiers' fair eyes might inspect these lines, for it is still to be seen whether the bearer of this letter, a Swiss journalist from Bâle who brought me news of the International, will reach London safe and sound. . . .

Letter from Élisabeth Dmitrieff to the General Council of the International in London, 24 April 1871: *Lettres de communards*, pp. 36–37, abridged.

Demand for free producers' co-operatives

We consider that the only way to reorganize labour so that the worker enjoys the product of his work is by forming free producers' co-operatives which would run the various industries and share the profits.

These co-operatives would deliver Labour from capitalist exploitation and thus enable the workers to control their own affairs. They would also facilitate urgently needed reforms in techniques of production and in the social relations of workers, as follows:

a The diversification of work within each trade to counter the harmful effects on body and mind of continually repeating the same manual operation;

b A reduction of working hours to prevent physical exhaustion leading to loss of mental faculties;

c The abolition of all competition between men and women workers since their interests are absolutely identical and their solidarity is essential to the success of the final and universal strike of Labour against Capital;

And therefore:

1 Equal pay for equal hours worked;

2 A federation of the various sections of the trades on a local and international level to facilitate the sale and exchange of products by centralizing the international interests of the producers.

The general development of these producers' co-operatives calls for:

1 Propaganda and organization among the working masses; every co-operative member shall therefore be expected to join the International Working Men's Association;

2 Financial aid from the State for the setting up of these co-operatives in the form of a social loan repayable in yearly instalments at 5 per cent interest.

We also believe that in the social order of the past women's work has been particularly subject to exploitation and therefore urgently needs to be reorganized.

Given the present situation, with poverty increasing at a terrifying rate because of the unjustified cessation of all work, it is to be feared that the women of Paris, having had their revolutionary moment, will relapse under the pressure of continuous hardship to the passive and more or less reactionary role that the social order of the past had cut out for them. This would endanger the revolutionary and international interests of the peoples of the world and consequently the Commune.

For these reasons the Central Committee of the Women's Union asks the Commune's Commission of Labour and Exchange to entrust it with the reorganization and allocation of women's work in Paris and to begin by placing it in charge of military supplies. Since this work is naturally not sufficient to employ the majority of women the federated producers' co-operatives should be given the necessary funds to take over those factories and workshops abandoned by the bourgeois where work is mainly carried out by women. . . .

Address from the Central Committee of the Women's
Union for the Defence of Paris and for Aid to the
Wounded to the Commission of Labour and Exchange:
A.H.G., Ly 23, abridged.

49 *The debate on bakers' night-work*

The Chairman – The agenda calls for a discussion on the Mont de Piété.[1]
J.-B. Clément – I asked for the floor on a procedural motion. Yesterday the owners of the bakeries held a meeting on the question of night-work; the bakery workers have threatened to smash their windows, and tonight in the 3rd arrondissement there is a danger of this happening. The employers were concerned about this and Citizen Paschal Grousset told them that the decree we enacted would be suspended until the 15th of next month. If you do not issue them with an official notice to post up on their doors there will undoubtedly be disturbances in the 3rd arrondissement tonight. In my opinion this decree was voted on rather impulsively and I ask that we take a formal decision on this matter.
Demay – The owners of the bakeries held a meeting yesterday in the 3rd arrondissement. The ask that night-work continue for a few more days so that the necessary leavens be prepared. After that, they decided, the decree would be observed.
Billioray – I do not think this calls for discussion; it is a matter for the Executive Commission. We should not have meddled in this question; it is the business solely of the interested parties.

136   [1] The state pawnshop.

Viard – I support Citizen Billioray's conclusions, especially at the present stage. This is a serious matter. Seventy bakery workers came earlier today to see Citizen Treilhard in protest against the situation you have created. It is not up to us to intervene in a matter between employers and workers, and I ask that the decree be revoked.

Avrial – The Executive Commission enacted this decree on the express demand of the bakery workers. They had been holding meetings for some time; you were not at these meetings and you do not realize how long they have been asking for this decree. They would have forced the employers to apply it by striking, but journeymen bakers cannot go on strike; the State prohibits it. Their work is immoral; we cannot divide society into two classes and force these workers, who are men like ourselves, to work only at night and never see the light of day. If you change your decision now the employers will still have all the advantages on their side. How many of your employers are there? A few of them may be objecting, but revoke the decree and you will have even more protests from the workers. The Executive Commission, in passing this decree, was acting in a spirit of justice.

Varlin – I entirely agree with Avrial. I shall abstain from speaking.

Ledroit – I am not of the opinion of Billioray and others who say that we ought not to meddle in these affairs. This is a social and humanitarian question. Bakery work can very well be done by day with the agreement of workers and employers. This is their particular concern and we ought not to meddle in it; but over and above this is the question that has just been brought to our attention, that bakery workers are not allowed to strike. It is therefore urgent that we be concerned with this question since they cannot stand up for their own rights.

Varlin – I asked for the floor on a point of order. I think it is useless to prolong the debate since the Commune has abolished night-work, unless someone formally asks for the decree to be revoked.

Theisz – No one is asking you to revoke the decree. You are only being asked that it be postponed for two or three days.

The Chairman – As I was on my way here I was assailed by eight or ten employers who seemed to want to help you make up your minds. They merely asked that the decree be suspended so that they could take stock of the new situation. I would now like to consult the Assembly on whether it will give Citizen Frankel the floor, since I believe he is one of the signatories of the decree.

Frankel – While I accept the principle of the decree I do not think its form is suitable. We should have made clear to the population of Paris what our motives were in passing such a decree. There are workers among us, Varlin, Malon, etc., who have been concerned as long as I have with social affairs; we should have been consulted, especially since the Commission 137 of Labour and Exchange had been giving this important question special consideration. Before passing a decree of this nature one ought to make sure there is an urgent need for social reform in a particular trade; the needs of the public must be considered and the people informed, so that they fully understand the benefits of the reform you are carrying out. You must explain why you are ordering this change from night- to day-work. You must point out that the class of bakery workers is the most unfortunate section of the proletariat; indeed you will not find a more under-privileged trade. Every day we are told that the workers should educate themselves, but how can you educate yourself when you work at night? The employers came today; there were five of them and they were not in agreement; they promised to side with justice, with the majority. I believe that the majority of the employers will agree with us when the reform is universally applied. You approve of the Executive Commission's decree, however imperfect; you must therefore agree with the reform we wish to introduce in the bakeries.

J.-B. Clément – In my opinion we cannot pass a decree such as this and then order that it be implemented at once. I agree with Frankel on moral grounds, but we must not forget either that for a very long time bakers have been organized to work at night and that it is impossible for them to alter their methods immediately. I could not for the life of me care whether we have freshly baked bread or not; what concerns me is that the bakers will find it impossible, practically speaking, to make these changes for some time. I therefore ask that the decree should not be enforced until the 15th of next month.

Vermorel – I contributed to the drafting of the decree and I must point out that it contains every guarantee of fairness. I am not surprised that the employers are objecting to it; they will complain whenever we threaten one of their privileges. We should therefore not be worried about this. However, since we must be practical, and since the question of competition between bakers must be considered, the latter have a right to ask us for a decree that safeguards their interests as far as possible. This is what we have done, by decreeing that the night is to end at 5 a.m., which enables fresh bread to be delivered at 8 o'clock in the morning. This ought to suffice, and to put things off until the 15th would be to sacrifice the interests of the workers to those of the employers. It would be against all principles of justice and human rights if we were to allow a worthwhile class of workers to remain outcasts of society for the benefit of the aristocracy of the belly.

Billioray – I am opposed to all these rules and regulations you seem to want to institute. How are you going to check that the bakers really start work at 5 and that some will not start at 4? Let the workers themselves defend their rights against the employers; at present they are strong enough to do what-

138 ever they like.

Malon – I have little to add to what Frankel has said. I do not think we can go back on our decision; it would be a retrograde step, for the decree is a fair one. In the provinces the bread is baked by day; in some country places it is even baked weekly and it is just as good. In Paris it is baked by night, as Vermorel rightly pointed out, merely in the interests of the aristocracy of the belly. The bakery owners cannot object to the speed with which this measure has been taken. It has been under study for two years and they must have expected a decision sooner or later. We are told that we should not be concerned with these social matters: I must say that up to now the State has intervened often enough against the workers; the least it can do now is to intervene in their favour.

Theisz – Our role in this affair should have been to listen to the interested parties. Were the employers consulted? No, they were not! We cannot condemn one of the parties without giving them a hearing. I agree that night-work is a bad thing. These workers ought not to be forced, like miners, to do a form of work condemned by civilization. But it does not follow that we have a right to pass a decree on the matter. Let us send for the employers and the workers and let us say to the former: here are the complaints made by the workers; discuss them among yourselves and if you, the employers, do not wish to yield to them, if you threaten us with closing down your shops, then we will resort to requisition. We will take over your businesses and employ the workers ourselves in exchange for fair remuneration. This is what we should have done rather than take decisions on the matter ourselves. . . .

Oudet – I agree with Citizen Theisz. Before passing the decree we should have consulted both workers and employers to obtain all the necessary information.

Frankel – I have already said, and I now repeat, that the decree passed by the Executive Commission was inadequate, because it was incomprehensible to the majority of those who have been concerned with social affairs for a long time. Nonetheless I support it because I feel that it is the only truly socialist decree passed by the Commune; the other decrees may be more adequately formulated but none is so frankly social in character. We are here not only to deal with the usual business of a municipal council but to make social reforms (*Hear, hear!*). To carry out these social reforms, ought we to consult the employers first? No! Were the employers consulted in '92? Was the nobility consulted? Of course not! I have accepted no other mandate than to defend the proletariat, and when a reform is just I accept it and carry it out without worrying about consulting the employers. The measure decreed is fair; we must therefore defend it (*Applause*). . . .

The debate in the Commune on bakers' night-work,
28 April 1871: *P.V.C.*, vol. i, pp. 538–43, abridged.

Part Ten: The Commune – 'Festival of the Oppressed'

The experience of a revolution culminates in a sense of excitement, a sense of the complete opening up of the future. The symbolist poet Villiers de l'Isle-Adam, who wrote for the Commune paper Le Tribun du Peuple *under the pseudonym of Marius, was not alone in depicting Paris under the Commune as a festive city (Document 50); the young ex-army officer Louis Barron, who arrived in Paris to join what he called 'the social revolution', did so too (Document 51). He also remarked upon the unwillingness of the Parisian population to spoil the pleasure of feeling that the city was their own by facing up to the grim likelihood of defeat and its consequences (Document 52). Jules Vallès had described the proclamation of the Commune as a festival (see Document 13 above), and during the Commune there were concerts (Documents 53 and 54), and monuments of the imperial past were ceremoniously destroyed (Document 55). A local committee decided to signify its rejection of the death penalty by publicly burning a newly made guillotine (Document 56). The Commune itself debated the issues of censorship and State support of the theatre (Document 57); and the artists, under the presidency of Gustave Courbet, who had been elected to the Commune in the April by-elections, formed themselves into an Artists' Federation to oppose State control of artistic patronage (Document 58). A similar attempt to break away from the dominance of the École des Beaux Arts and the Academy had been proposed during the 1848 revolution without success.*

50 Paris as a festival

Would you believe it? Paris is fighting and singing! Paris is about to be attacked by a ruthless and furious army and she laughs! Paris is hemmed in on all sides by trenches and fortifications, and yet there are corners within these formidable walls where people still laugh!

Paris does not only have soldiers, she has singers too. She has both cannons and violins; she makes both Orsini[1] bombs and music. The clash of cymbals can be heard in the dreadful silence between rounds of firing, and merry dance airs mingle with the rattle of American machine-guns.

That is the way it is. As we all know, this is an amazing city.

During the siege of Lerida the noblemen of the Great Condé's army had

---

[1] A reference to Felice Orsini, who attempted to assassinate the Emperor in
140   January 1858.

Ticket admitting Gustave Lemaire, a member of a Paris section of the International, to the Place Vendôme to watch the demolition of the Column, 16 May 1871.

the fanciful idea of hiring fiddlers to play a fashionable dance tune while the attack was being launched. Beside themselves with fear, the fiddlers nevertheless did their duty; so did the gentlemen; the tune was played to the end and Lerida was taken and sacked from top to bottom.

The story went down in history. The noblemen and the fiddlers both became famous for their bravery, but now they have been outdone by far!

One is indeed given to laughter and song after escaping imminent death. The certitude that tomorrow will bring further dangers does not prevent us from making the most of our brief moment of respite. One cannot always be heroic; it is a good thing to descend from time to time from our epic heights.

Paris would indeed be a strange sight for someone suddenly finding himself in our midst, not knowing anything about our struggles and aspirations and looking objectively at our city that has become so mysterious and impenetrable since this vicious blockade.

At every step he would come across some astonishing spectacle. Where he might expect to see a people in mourning, roaming grief-stricken among the empty streets and squares of their depopulated city, instead he would find them peacefully going about their affairs, bent, according to their fancy or the time of day, on either business or pleasure.

He would be particularly amazed by the music-halls. However, if he reflected for a moment he would have to admit that it is good that the laughter of the people, like a ray of sunlight in a thunderstorm, should ring out now and then amid the turmoil of civil war.

The atmosphere we breathe is laden with hatred. The sky above us is no longer blue, its azure is marred by the smoke of burning villages; even the sun's rays come to us through the red glow of shell and machine-gun fire. Laughter alone, the eternal prerogative of man, survives, splendid and invincible, in a world of ruins.

If we should ever lose this powerful tonic that warms our veins and multiplies our strength tenfold, then we shall be diminished, weakened, spent. Paris is the city of heroism and of laughter; it gave birth to Pantagruel and to the Declaration of the Rights of Man. Let him laugh heartily, the giant loved by Rabelais and feared by Robespierre!

What better proof of strength than our peals of laughter echoing the exploding shells all around us that threaten at any moment to bury us alive under the smouldering ruins of our homes? This is our ultimate, invincible weapon: no one can take it from us.

Nothing could be better calculated to throw the enemy off course, to insult them and to make them so utterly weary that they will realize the uselessness of their destructive task. No more effective weapon could ever be found than the laughter of the people ringing out joyfully in the midst of the gloomy crowd like a shaft of lightning in a terrible storm.

No better reply could be made to our stubborn enemies' ceaseless cannonade than the refrain that a thousand voices intone every night in the twenty music-halls of Paris:

> '*The peoples of the world are brothers to us,*
> *Our enemies are the Versaillais.*'

Villiers de l'Isle-Adam on Paris as a festival: reprinted in
Le Mercure de France, 1 August 1953, pp. 593–5.

51 *The excitement of the revolution*

Even in these fearful times I enjoy public festivities, where the real people, moved by lofty ideals or generous sentiments, reveal their naïve and playful curiosity, their enthusiasm, their spontaneous kindness. One cannot be bored in their company. Never having been dulled by a surfeit of pleasure, they are entertained by anything; to arouse their enthusiasm, provoke their laughter or their tears, a word is enough, a comic turn, a cry of pain; immediately their features, their eyes, their gestures become animated and exalted. Their response is so vivid and contagious that it is impossible to remain indifferent; one must either avoid them or become totally involved.

In these solemn ceremonies, these festivities, these battles joyously fought, are born the great and sublime movements that cause people to break out of their habits and set their sights on a new ideal. The educated and positive-thinking, the sceptical and the spiritually inclined, all find themselves involved in spite of themselves, carried along with the common multitude. This is how viable revolutions begin and develop. One returns from such exalted experiences as one would awake from a dream, but the memory remains of a brief moment of ecstasy, an illusion of fraternity.

Barron, *Sous le drapeau rouge*, pp. 111–12.

The revolutionaries' optimism

If I were at all capable of reflection I would be quick to realize the folly of this hopeless struggle. I would cast off my rebel's uniform and humbly admit that we do not stand a chance. The Parisian movement is not impelled by feverish enthusiasm, illusions of dedication or mad ambitions; it is carried along purely by its own momentum, and oddly enough I have become deeply involved in it, almost without my knowledge. I recklessly allow myself to be swept along in its current; my intelligence lies dormant. I hardly ever think of the dangers of the morrow.

As for the threatening notices that Monsieur Thiers's government is clandestinely posting up in the streets, they amuse rather than frighten me. Their official jargon is an object of fun, a meaningless threat. Everyone else reads the posters and, like me, they laugh, shrug their shoulders, crack jokes. Would you like to know why? Because Paris seems literally impregnable; one feels so secure and comfortable here. And then the fine weather – which is playing into the hands of the Versaillais – is so balmy, so caressing that it softens the very marrow of the bones and soothes away all memory, all resentment of the bad old days of the Great Siege. We have become luke-warm characters inclined to sentimentality.

Eating and drinking their fill, making love, the Parisians under the second siege have no energy left to imagine, even vaguely, the horrific consequences of defeat. In order to forewarn the population and prepare them for resistance tracts have been distributed, reminding them of the bloody days of June 1848, but of no avail; they are no longer in a state to believe 143 the dreadful tales of summary executions, mass imprisonment in fortified dungeons and prison ships, deportations. This is how a delightful climate will affect brains that are naturally disposed to frivolity.

I was told by federal troops: 'You see, if the Versaillais enter Paris it is the members of the Commune and the Central Committee who had better beware! The deserters too. They will be shot, but us, poor devils, ordinary workers, what do you expect them to do with us? Sack us, that's all.'

So I go back to my post to observe the game of social warfare. And I must admit that the cheerful bravado of the participants, their frivolous chatter, their wildly ostentatious dress, their taste for brilliant colours, plumed hats and impassioned speeches all help to distract me from my brooding fears. Events take place, the drama unfolds, and no one is worried or upset. Our appetites are good. Our laughter comes easily. We feel quite at home in our childish and dangerous world of make-believe.

We do not take ourselves seriously – on the surface at least – but it is not impossible that in moments of solitude, where calm brings back a sense of reality, more than one of us is given to wondering about the consequences of his daring escapade, about his future and perhaps even his survival. Tomorrow, the day after tomorrow, in a week or a month, what then? After such a prolonged and radical break with the social order, what are we to expect of those who defeat us? The firing-squad, imprisonment, deportation? Or if by miracle we should escape – banishment, a miserable existence abroad, and later, if there is an amnesty, a permanent loss of civil rights in our own country?

This vague and awesome threat is ever-present; we may think of it for a moment, shudder for a second, but most of the time we put it out of our minds. Things will work out, we think comfortingly. From this secure position the actors in the great military drama of the Commune, glorying in their role, are able to throw themselves into it without any self-consciousness, with perfect ease and marvellous gusto, the hallmarks of an obvious vocation. The plot develops, thickens; scenes follow in rapid succession, tableaux appear and disappear, the ending will soon be revealed. Meanwhile the cannon punctuate this amazing show of merriment and sentimentality. How could one imagine that such a varied, entertaining play could ever have a tragic end?

Barron, pp. 83–87.

53 A concert

Here at last is the singer we have been waiting for all evening: the most
popular prima donna, the star of the show, la Bordas, magnificent in her

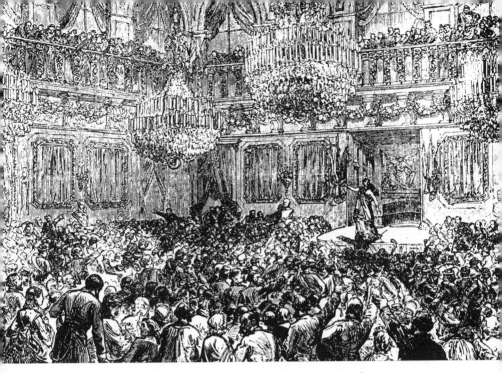

Amid the imperial pomp of the Tuileries Palace, a popular singer rouses the revolutionary fervour of her audience.

flowing robe draped with a scarlet sash, her long hair framing her beautiful, broad face, her generous bosom half exposed, her arms bare. She stands like a warlike apparition . . . a goddess of Liberty from the popular *quartiers*, born of the poet's imagination and of the people's too, whose ideal she personifies. Our statuesque idol moves slowly and majestically, her great eyes mesmerizing the audience, who follow her every gesture with rapt attention.

In the folds of her robe she carries illusion, faith, hope, enthusiasm. Let her sing, let her sing the song that has made her famous, *La Canaille* [*The · Rabble*], and every heart will beat in unison!

La Canaille is the revolutionary anthem of modern times, a vindication, a glorification of the oppressed worker. Just as the Dutch rebels of the sixteenth century took the name of Beggars, with which the Spaniards reviled them, so the insurrectionists of the days of the Empire, the victims of the terror of June 1848, the men in overalls pledged to a hatred of the 'truncheon brigade', the grotesque fops of 1869, chose to calls themselves the Rabble, a name thrown in their face as the ultimate insult.

One really must hear this anthem bellowed in la Bordas's formidable, 145 brazen voice, with fierce passion and a fury that inflames the soul. She lends every line of the simple little song a warlike vigour and resonance; the proud refrain,

> They're the Rabble!
> Well – I'm one of them!

unfurls from her tongue like a scarlet banderilla waved in front of a bull. She wraps herself in the folds of a red flag, pointing with outstretched arm to the invisible enemy, urging us to pursue him with our hatred and crush him mercilessly. The crowd is in raptures; they recognize in these wild strains their inspiration and their innermost feelings. They clap and stamp their feet, rise in frenzied applause, shouting 'Bravo! Encore!' The prima donna takes up the last verse once more. . . .

Barron, pp. 122–24, abridged.

54 *Dr Rousselle's poster*

People!

The gold that glitters on these walls[1] is the product of your toil! For long enough your work has nourished and your blood has quenched the thirst of the insatiable monster of Monarchy.

Today the Revolution has made you free; at last you may claim your rightful property. This land is yours. But retain your dignity, for you are strong, and be watchful, for the tyrants must never return.

Poster displayed by Dr Rousselle during the concerts at
the Tuileries: D'Alméras, *La Vie Parisienne pendant le siège
et sous la Commune*, p. 452.

55 *The destruction of the Vendôme Column*

An enormous crowd fills the Rue de la Paix. Above their heads, against a beautifully clear sky – a *Floréal*[2] sky – the column soars. The red flag flies from the railing at the top, gently flapping against Caesar's face. Three cables hang from the summit, linked to the capstan that will later revolve and pull the monument towards it.

A murmur rises from the crowd. Has the column's last moment arrived?

---

[1] The brocaded walls of the Tuileries Palace, used for concerts by the Communards and burnt down at the end of the Commune.

[2] The eighth month (20 April to 19 May) of the republican calendar instituted in 1793.

146

'Quick, let's go', said Vermeersch.[1] 'It looks as though it's going to start.'

As we begin to plough our way through the seething mass of people we try to catch what those nearest to us are saying. There are few recriminations; the dominant mood seems to be one of anxiety about the crash.

'It will burst the sewers of the Rue de la Paix,' says one man.

'What if it knocks down the houses in the square?', says another.

Of the column itself, of Napoleon, the Great Army, Austerlitz, not a word.

The shops are closed. Strips of paper have been pasted across the windows to protect them against the shock.

At last we reach the barrier that fences off the square. We show our cards to the sentry. . . .

The hall of the Ministry of Justice is packed with people; the balcony is already full. Through the wide-open windows we have a view of the square and the multitude of uniforms. The sun is burning hot on the cobble-stones. Leaning against the column railings is a young commander of one of the many battalions, the Avengers, the Defenders or the Turcos, with his red tunic and triple row of glittering braid.

At the corners of the square the brass instruments of the bands gleam in the sunlight.

Below us stand five or six members of the Commune: Miot, with his tall stature and long white beard; Ferré, a little man with a black beard hiding most of his face, an aquiline nose and very black eyes that are soft and yet gleam strangely from behind his glasses.

On the pedestal of the column half a dozen men are having an animated discussion, looking up inquiringly at the place where the column has been partially sawn through.

'We need a bit more sawing,' orders one of them.

The saw goes into action, biting a little further into the column and letting off a puff of white dust.

'All right, we can pull now.'

The time is half past three.

They give the column a tug – Crack! The capstan breaks and the cables slacken. Murmurs of disappointment. The word goes round that people have been injured.

---

[1] Vermeersch and Vuillaume (the author of this extract) were two of the three editors of the popular Communard paper, *Le P're Dûchene*. The Vendôme Column had been built by the first Napoleon to glorify the victories of the Grand Army. With the revival of Bonapartism in the 1840s it had become a symbol of the Napoleonic legend, and in 1864 Napoleon III had had a new statue of his uncle, dressed in a Roman toga, placed on the top. Republicans hated the column as a symbol of militarism and despotism. It was restored after the defeat of the Commune, the unfortunate, and innocent, Gustave Courbet being charged with the cost; he was forced to go into exile in Switzerland to avoid paying.

The painter Gustave Courbet, who in 1848 and 1871 tried to ally art to revolution. After the Commune the Third Council of War quite unfairly declared him financially responsible for the replacement of the demolished Vendôme Column, and he was forced to flee to Switzerland to avoid payment.

Fallen monument of Empire: the shattered remnants of the Vendôme Column.

New pulleys are fetched. . . . Over an hour's wait.

Someone wheels the astronomers' telescope into a safe place; it had been left out in the open and was about to become the innocent victim of the demolition.

A quarter past five. The men on the pedestal are driving wedges into the incision at the base of the column. The monster refuses to budge. To entertain the crowd the bands play the *Marseillaise*. The Rue de Castiglione and the Rue de la Paix are a swarming mass of people hemmed in by the barriers.

The bands suddenly stop playing. An officer has climbed to the top. He takes down the red flag and replaces it with a tricolour. A shudder runs through me – the column looked as though it were shifting.

The officer has disappeared now, he is climbing down the inner staircase. What if the column were to fall right now with him inside? No – here he is.

I let out a sigh of relief; what an insane thought to have! Ah, the column is still standing firm; they will obviously tauten the cables in vain.

Then suddenly, there it is, like the flap of a gigantic bird's wing, a huge zig-zag through the air! Ah, I shall never forget that colossal shadow falling across my eyes!

Flop! A cloud of smoke.

All is over. The column lies on the ground, split open, its stony entrails exposed to the wind. Caesar is lying prostrate and headless. The laurel-wreathed head has rolled like a pumpkin into the gutter. The bronze statue of Victory is intact. By evening it had disappeared.

Vuillaume, *Mes Cahiers rouges au temps de la Commune*,
vol. v., pp. 174–8, abridged.

Since it is impossible to get objective information owing to the varying newspaper reports and the malicious rumours spread by the reactionaries, I would like to draw your attention to the facts contained in the following document:

An inquiry produced evidence that the Versailles Government had ordered and paid for the manufacture of guillotines, and had recently recommended that an improved guillotine be completed as soon as possible, giving details of the design, the craftsmen to be employed, the tools and finally the *corpus delicti*.

This improved guillotine was requisitioned, together with the standard instrument. The sub-committee met for deliberation and decided that both instruments of execution were to be burned in a public place, this event to be proclaimed by the local town crier.

Here is the text of the notice that was displayed:

Citizens,

We have been informed of the construction of a new type of guillotine that was commissioned by the odious government – one that is easier to transport and speedier.

The Sub-Committee of the 11th Arrondissement has ordered the seizure of these servile instruments of monarchist domination and has voted that they be destroyed once and forever.

They will therefore be burned at ten o'clock on 6 April 1871, on the Place de la Mairie, for the purification of the Arrondissement and the consecration of our new freedom.

Burning the guillotine in the 11th arrondissement,
6 April 1871: *J.O.*, 10 April 1871.

57 *The control of theatres*

The Chairman – At the beginning of the session Citizen Vaillant asked that we deal with the question of the theatres. He is anxious that we hold a debate on this matter.

Cournet – In my opinion the theatres are a means of popular education and as such they should be brought under the Education Commission.

The Chairman – I must admit that I do not see the connection between education and choreography. However, I will read out Vaillant's motion.

'In accordance with the principles established by the First Republic and expressed in the law of Germinal 11, Year II,[1]

[1] 31 March 1794.

The guillotine – 'servile instrument of monarchist domination' – is burnt beneath the statue of Voltaire in the 11th arrondissement.

'The Commune decrees:

'The theatres are the responsibility of the Education Delegation, as far as their organization, direction and administration are concerned. The Delegation is to put an end to the system of commercial exploitation of theatres by directors or firms and replace it as rapidly as possible by a system of co-operative associations.

É. Vaillant.'

Pyat – I do not understand Citizen Vaillant's demands, nor do I understand Citizen Cournet's. In my opinion State intervention in the running of theatres is no more defensible than in the world of literature. When the State is still in its infancy the theatres need some form of protection, a Richelieu or some such patron, but in a free country that professes individual liberty and freedom of conscience to place the theatres under the tutelage of the State is un-republican. One is perfectly entitled to keep an eye on the way people use their minds, but to instruct them how to use them is a form of tyranny that is not only intolerable but fatal to the development of thought.

The glory of French theatre is precisely that it has freed itself from patronage. When Molière founded his theatre an official theatre was already in existence, but this was not Molière's. In fact he set up his theatre right opposite the one subsidized and patronized by the State. I am not opposed 151 for the present to the theatres being closely supervised, but I defend the absolute right of individual thought to express itself in whatever form it chooses.

Vaillant – I do not think Citizen Pyat has understood the meaning of my proposal. The First Republic did not think of the freedom of theatres in the way we think of it today. It managed them in a somewhat dictatorial way. It demanded, for example, that they perform such and such a play three times a week. But remember that whenever we are true to principles of justice we are always acting in the name of freedom. And when the State bears the name of Commune it should intervene often, in the name of justice and freedom. Not only is this intervention highly advisable, it is also an important political act. Moreover, it is highly advisable that the Police should not meddle in social affairs. We must aim to build up socialist institutions everywhere.

What makes the Revolution of the nineteenth century so distinctive is that it is based on the theory that wherever a product exists the producer should be fully compensated. Exploitation in art is perhaps even more extreme than in the workshop; all theatre personnel are exploited from top to bottom. The dancer has to sell herself in order to survive. People are being cheated all along the line. We must introduce a régime of equality in the theatres, the system of co-operative associations. The Police should be concerned solely with safeguarding morality and with matters of security. I suggest that we set up a special committee for the arts. The Police obviously have no place on such a committee, which by right comes under the Education Commission. It is the duty of the present theatre administration to transform the system of private ownership and privilege into a system of co-operative associations wholly in the hands of the performers.

Félix Pyat – I am delighted Citizen Vaillant has agreed that the theatres are a case for co-operative associations. An association is better than a board of directors and far better than a single director. But I would like to point out that you cannot prevent directorships in private business; you have no right to say that no citizen of Paris has the right to open a theatre. I will now join you on your own ground: if you wish to introduce associations in theatres subsidized by the State, then you are within your right since it is you who are paying. But first of all I would like to question whether it is really necessary for the State to support a theatre, and whether the farmers of Berry should be made to pay for ballet dancers. I think it absurd myself.

We are communalists and federalists, as we have said before. Well then, if the Paris Commune chooses to spend money on an opera-house let it not force the farmers of Beauce to share the costs! The Commune ought not to tyrannize the country people into paying taxes for a theatre on the Paris boulevards. I am thoroughly opposed to the whole of France paying for a Parisian opera-house. If later on you should see the need for a communal opera-house, and I for my part do not, then let the Commune pay for it. Then and only then will you have the right to impose on your actors whatever form of organization you choose.

As for patronage or any kind of deliberate influence on the arts, this is in my opinion an attack on the freedom of human thought; at the same time it represents an inconsistency on your part. There should no more be a State literature or a State science than a State religion. The academies of medicine or music should disappear totally in their present form; they are a form of tyranny exerted in the arts, science and literature which is exactly the same as religious tyranny.

Judging from what I have seen in other countries, I have no hesitation in saying that if science in France is lagging behind the times, if its genius is inferior to that of other nations, this is due above all to the harmful practice of patronage. What remarkable works have we produced since we have had a Théâtre Français, since a gentleman of the Privy Chamber became responsible for the Comédie Française? We have only produced insignificant things, mere abortions of art. England has produced Newton – does it have academies subsidized by the State? Not at all! Its seats of learning are all organized on a local basis; they are independent but federalized and they derive their superiority precisely from this freedom. I therefore protest against the system of patronage which has been suggested to you, since I am absolutely convinced that our literature and science, which have been dead since the eighteenth century, are not going to be revived with all the good will in the world unless they are allowed absolute freedom.

Langevin – I do not agree with Citizen Pyat. If the theatre is an instrument of education I would like to see the Commune exercising a strict and serious control over this aspect of learning. In my opinion the reason for the poor progress of literature is not to be sought in excessive protection but rather in the tolerance shown to bad literature. I am therefore in favour of control of the theatres by the Commune.

Vésinier – I would like to read out a motion:

'The Commune decrees:

'1 All subsidies and monopolies in the theatre are to be abolished.

'2 The theatres are to have absolute freedom.

'3 Any crimes or misdemeanours to do with theatrical performances are to be treated as crimes and misdemeanours of common law and are to be controlled and punished as such.

Vésinier'

There can no more be theatrical, journalistic or literary misdemeanours than there can be crimes or misdemeanours of thought. Crimes can be occasioned by certain plays, but these are common law crimes and come under ordinary jurisdiction. What we want is freedom, the right to do whatever is not harmful to other people, not a regulated freedom governed 153 by special laws. This is the reason for the motion I have just read out to you.

Vaillant – Citizens, we ought to be concerned with politics and not with metaphysics. We do not wish to interfere with freedom, but we have set ourselves a task of reorganization which ought to be comprehensive. Theatres are not only mouths but stomachs too. They involve people who earn an enormous amount and others who do not earn enough. We are faced with conditions of a moral and material order that require regulating by the Commune. Of course we are not in favour of *state art*. We are only concerned at present with public security and morality. We must put an end to all forms of exploitation. Who is to be in charge of this task? The delegation immediately responsible, until such time as you create a delegation with overall powers to liquidate the old society. My motion is thus an organizational proposal.

Vésinier – I withdraw my motion and I request that it should not appear in the *Journal Officiel*. We should not sit here talking about the theatre while we are being bombarded.

Pyat – During the period of fighting I accept that one should have, as in Year II, an absolute right to control all expression, whatever the medium, be it the Press, the theatre or the paint-brush. If you use these media to incite people to civil war then you ought to be suppressed. But I still maintain everything I have said for the future. (*Cries of 'Take a vote!'*)

The motion is read again.

Vésinier – I would like to table an amendment to the proposed decree of Citizen Vaillant. This is what I suggest: 'Theatrical monopolies and subsidies are to be abolished.'

Pyat – But Vaillant's proposal will mean that a director will be prevented from opening a theatre because he believes that theatres can only be run by co-operative associations.

Frankel – I agree with both, Citizen Vaillant and Citizen Félix Pyat. Let me explain. I think it would be most unfavourable to the socialist cause we are defending for the theatres to be dependent on any committee. The theatres ought to be run by the members of the co-operative associations. It is up to them to appoint their directors. However, I do not agree with Citizen Félix Pyat that the State ought never to encourage a co-operative association or intervene in theatrical matters. When the powers that be are bent on keeping the minds of the public in a hothouse, as under Napoleon III, they obviously have no right to intervene in the people's affairs, which are foreign to them. But when the State can be said to represent the mass of individuals it is its duty to concern itself with literature as well as education. We were told that thought should be free, that minds should not be under any tutelage. Let me quote the example of two men: Diderot, who was patronized by Russia, and Voltaire, who was the protégé of Frederick of Prussia.

To sum up, I think the theatres should be placed under the supervision of the Education Delegation, who will provide the co-operative associations with all possible support.

The Chairman – Citizen Vaillant has withdrawn part of his draft. He has retained the organizational aspect which he could also drop in my opinion. This being so I think we can take a vote on the motion.

Vésinier – I wish to remind you that I tabled an amendment.

Frankel – Does Citizen Vésinier mean by the word *subsidy* contained in his amendment, a credit made available to co-operative associations?

Vésinier – Yes. The co-operative associations may be encouraged financially, but any association can be formed freely without a subsidy or monopoly necessarily being granted.

Citizen Vaillant's decree is amended, put to the vote and passed.

The debate in the Commune on the control of theatres,
19 May 1871: *P.V.C.*, vol. ii, pp. 426–30.

8 *Formation of an Artists' Federation*

Yesterday at two o'clock in the main amphitheatre of the École de Médecine a meeting of artists was organized by M. Courbet under the auspices of the Commune. The hall was packed and the various arts were well represented. . . .

M. Courbet chaired the meeting, accompanied by M. Moulin and M. Pottier. He opened the meeting by reading the report of a sub-committee which he had drafted himself. . . .

The idea that artists should be responsible for their own affairs seemed to be the main point of the sub-committee's report. It suggested that a *federation* of Parisian artists be set up, to include all artists exhibiting their works in Paris.

Paris Artists' Federation

The artists of Paris who supported the principles of the Communal Republic will form themselves into a federation. This association of the creative minds of the city will be based on the following ideas:

The free development of art without government protection or special privileges.

Equal rights for all members of the Federation.

The independence and dignity of each artist to be guaranteed by the group as a whole through the intermediary of a committee elected by all member artists.

This committee is to strengthen solidarity between members and provide unity of action. . . .

Definition of responsibilities

The realm of the arts will be controlled by the artists, who will have the following duties:

To conserve the heritage of the past;

To facilitate the creation and exhibition of contemporary works;

To stimulate future creation through art education.

Historical buildings and museums

The historical buildings of artistic value and the museums and buildings of Paris containing galleries, collections or libraries of works of art, unless privately owned, will be entrusted to the Committee for conservation and administration.

The Committee will compile, preserve, revise and complete the plans, inventories, repositories and catalogues of these establishments. It will make these documents available to the public for purposes of study and information.

It will survey the buildings, suggest any necessary repairs and report frequently to the Commune on any work undertaken.

It will appoint administrators, secretaries, archivists and wardens, selected on the basis of ability and trustworthiness, to run these establishments and to organize exhibitions (see below).

These officials may be dismissed on grounds of negligence, incompetence or misconduct.

Exhibitions

The Committee will organize municipal, national and international exhibitions in Paris.

Where a national or international exhibition is held outside Paris the Committee will send a delegation on the spot to represent the interests of Parisian painters.

The Committee will only accept works signed by their authors. These may be original creations or transpositions of creative works from one medium into another, such as engraved reproductions of paintings etc.

The Committee is strongly opposed to purely commercial exhibitions where the name of the printer or manufacturer is given more prominence than that of the genuine creator.

No prizes will be awarded.

Routine work commissioned by the Commune will be shared out among artists nominated by a vote of all Committee members. Exceptional commissions will be awarded by competition.

Education

The Committee will supervise the teaching of drawing and modelling in
municipal elementary and technical schools, the teachers being appointed

by competitive examination. The Committee will encourage the introduction of rational, stimulating teaching methods, design the models used in the schools and recommend especially gifted students for further studies at the Commune's expense. . . .

Information

The Committee will publish an information journal entitled the *Official Journal of the Arts*.

This journal will be under the control and responsibility of the Committee; it will publicize artistic events and information useful to artists.

It will publish reports of the Committee's work, the minutes of its meetings, its budget and any informative statistics.

It will include a literary section devoted to dissertations in the field of aesthetics; all opinions and theories will be given an open hearing.

A progressive, independent and honest publication, the *Official Journal of the Arts* will be worthy of representing our new movement.

Arbitration

In all litigation involving the arts, the Committee, on the request of the interested parties, artists and others, will designate arbitrators to reconcile the parties.

On questions of principle and public interest the Committee will form itself into an arbitration council and its decisions will be reported in the *Official Journal of the Arts*.

Encouragement of individual projects

The Committee invites all citizens to submit to them proposals, projects, memoirs or communications concerning the development of the arts, the moral or intellectual emancipation of artists and the improvement of their material status.

It will inform the Commune of these projects and lend its support and collaboration in whatever schemes it considers practicable.

It will submit these projects to the approval of the public by publishing them in the *Official Journal of the Arts*.

Finally, by the pen and the pencil, by the popular reproduction of works of art and images of artistic and moral value in public places, right down to the remotest town halls, the Committee will work for cultural regeneration, the building of a communal heritage of beauty, the future development of art and the Universal Republic.

G. Courbet, Moulinet, Stephen Martin, Alexandre Jousse, Roszezench, Trichon, Dalou, Jules Héreau, C. Chabert, H. Dubois, A. Faleynière, Eugène Pottier, Perrin, A. Moulliard.

Report on the meeting held to form an Artists' Federation, 14 April 1871: *J.O.*, 15 April 1871, abridged.

Part Eleven: The Repression of the Commune

It took Thiers's government just over two months to build up, with the connivance of the Prussians, a fresh army with which to take Paris and put an end to the Commune. On Sunday 21 May the first detachments of Versailles troops entered the capital from the south-west at one of the many unguarded points. The news caught the Commune unawares, and most of the population was enjoying a Sunday promenade or, as it turned out, the last of the concerts in the Tuileries. The aged Jacobin, Charles Delescluze, who had taken over from Rossel as Delegate of War, simply issued a proclamation calling for the erection of barricades (Document 59), as did the Committee of Public Safety (Document 60). There was to be no organized defence of the city as a whole, and no plans had been made for this during the previous months. In any case, resort to the barricades had become the tradition of revolutions in nineteenth-century Paris (there had been no street barricades during the first Revolution), and no instructions were needed to produce piles of cobble-stones wherever one went (Document 61). Several appeals to the Versailles troops were published (e.g. Document 62) in the hope that they would fraternize, as they had done in March at the beginning of the Commune. But Thiers had been careful to keep this new army separate from the population, and it was made up of returned prisoners of war and recruits from the provinces who had had no contact with fevered Paris – unlike the troops used so unsuccessfully on 18 March, who had been billeted in the city and shared with the rest of the population in the rigours of the siege. Instead, in May, the army and the police mercilessly shot practically everyone in sight; Paris was put to the sack (Document 63), and the shootings continued well after the last of the barricades had fallen. Something in the order of 25,000 people were killed. The barricade was not really a serious form of defence and had only resulted in a similar massacre in the June 1848 uprising. At best barricades could check the troops and so give the insurgents time to try to win the soldiers over. Auguste Blanqui, having given thought to the problem in the 1860s, had warned against the danger of becoming 'shut up, each in his own quartier' ;[1] *and Engels also used the example of the Commune as a warning to the German Social Democratic Party in his 1895 Preface to Marx's* The Class Struggle in France. *Gustave Cluseret, who had been made a General for playing a minor role on the side of the North during the American Civil War and who was the first of the Commune's War Delegates, also published his reflections on the street fighting, which he may have seen but in which he certainly did not take part, having*

---

[1] Blanqui MSS., published in V. P. Volguine (ed.), *Textes Choisis*, Paris, 1955.

The final resistance. Above, passers-by help to build a barricade. Below, Paris
burns – on the left the Tuileries Palace, on the opposite bank government
buildings on the Quai d'Orsay.

disguised himself as a priest in order to avoid arrest (Document 64). Cluseret's com-
ments were later translated into Russian with a short commentary by Lenin and
published in Vperyod, 23–30 March 1905. Many public buildings as well as
private houses were burnt down by the Communards during their retreat across
Paris. This was partly a means of defence, but some fires, notably those at the
Tuileries Palace, the Prefecture of Police and probably the Hôtel de Ville were
started as symbolic acts linking the death of the Commune to earlier, historically
famous defences of a city under siege (Document 65). At the end of the last week in
May, Marshal MacMahon, the Commander-in-Chief of the army of Versailles,
announced that order was restored (Document 66).

59 Delescluze's proclamation

FRENCH REPUBLIC

LIBERTY   EQUALITY   FRATERNITY

PARIS COMMUNE

To the People of Paris,

To the National Guard,

CITIZENS,

Enough of militarism, no more staff-officers with gold-embroidered uniforms! Make way for the people, the bare-armed fighters! The hour of revolutionary war has struck.

The people know nothing of elaborate manœuvres, but when they have a rifle in their hands and cobble-stones under their feet they have no fear for the strategists of the monarchist school.

To arms! Citizens, to arms! It is a choice now, as you know, between conquering or falling into the merciless hands of the reactionaries and clericals of Versailles, those scoundrels who deliberately handed over France to the Prussians and are making us pay the ransom of their treachery.

If you are determined that the generous blood that has flowed like water these past six weeks should not have been shed in vain, if you wish to live in a free and egalitarian France, if you wish to spare your children the suffering and misery you have endured, then you must rise as one man. Faced with your formidable resistance, the enemy who flatters himself he will again submit you to his yoke will win no more than the shame of the useless crimes with which he has befouled himself for the past two months.

Citizens, your mandatories will fight beside you and die beside you if need be. In the name of glorious France, mother of all popular revolutions,

eternal home of those ideas of justice and solidarity which must and will be
the laws of the world, we exhort you to march against the enemy! Let your
revolutionary energy show them that Paris may be sold but it cannot yield
or be conquered!

The Commune counts on you, count on the Commune!

Proclamation by Charles Delescluze, the Commune's
Delegate of War, at the news of the entry of the
Versailles troops, 21 May 1871: *M.P.*, vol. ii, p. 558.

) *Proclamation by the Committee of Public Safety*

Citizens,

The Porte de Saint-Cloud – besieged on all four sides by the guns of the
Mont-Valérien, the Butte Mortemart, Moulineaux and the fort at Issy, all
delivered to the enemy through treachery – the Porte de Saint-Cloud has
been forced by the Versaillais, who have now occupied part of Paris.

This setback should not dishearten you but rather spur you to action. The
People, who dethrone monarchs, who destroy Bastilles, the People of '89
and '93, the People of the Revolution cannot lose in one day the freedom
they won on 18 March.

People of Paris, we cannot possibly abandon the struggle now, for it is the
struggle of the future against the past, of Liberty against tyranny, Equality
against monopoly, Fraternity against enslavement and the Solidarity of the
peoples of the world against the self-interest of the oppressors.

TO ARMS!

TO ARMS, then! Let Paris bristle with barricades, and from behind these
improvised ramparts let our war-cry ring out against the enemy, our cry
of pride, of defiance, but also of victory – for thanks to its barricades Paris
is impregnable.

Let all the cobble-stones in Paris be dug up, first because enemy projectiles
will do less damage if they fall on bare earth, and second because the cobbles
are our new means of defence and must be stacked up at intervals on the
balconies of upper stories.

Let revolutionary Paris, the Paris of *les grandes journées*, do its duty; the
Commune and the Committee of Public Safety will do theirs.

Proclamation to the people of Paris by the Committee of
Public Safety on the entry of the troops of Versailles:
J.O., 24 May 1871.

61 The barricades

Towards noon the general stupor gave way to a certain amount of activity.
Barricades were being built all over Paris. The 1871 barricade is a rather
meagre fortification: a wall of cobble-stones between $4\frac{1}{2}$ and 5 feet high
and 3 to $4\frac{1}{2}$ feet thick. It is sometimes faced or crenellated with cobbles.
Once taken, this paltry barrier works to the disadvantage of its defenders,
since its structure is similar on both sides.

Passers-by were stopped to help construct the barricades. A battalion of
National Guards occupied the area, and the sentries called on everyone
passing to contribute their cobble-stone willy-nilly to the defence effort.
This method is vexatious and inefficient; if the National Guards had put
themselves to the task they would have done it much faster and better in
spite of their laziness. . . .

In barricade fighting the Parisian finds an energy that he does not
possess when defending fortifications or fighting ordinary campaigns. The
possibility of fleeing, of escaping the consequences of defeat by returning
home, of taking up arms again whenever the time is right, gives him the
security that regular troops derive from marching in close formation and
rallying round the flag.

Because he wants to be able to retreat easily the soldier of the barricades
will not wear a uniform when he intends to engage in serious fighting. It
may seem paradoxical, but the uniform does in fact lessen the street
fighter's courage; men in overalls have far more energy, initiative and
military skill than National Guardsmen and especially officers of the
National Guard.

L.-N. Rossel's comments on the Paris barricades: Rossel,
pp. 275–77, abridged.

62 Appeal to the soldiers of Versailles

Soldiers of the Versailles Army,

We are family men.

We are fighting so that our children will never have to bend, as you must,
under military despotism.

One day you will have children too.

If you fire on the people today your sons will condemn you, as we
condemn the soldiers who massacred the people in June 1848 and December
1851.

Two months ago, on 18 March, your brothers of the Paris Army, bitterly resentful of the cowards who had betrayed France, fraternized with the people. We urge you to follow their example.

Soldiers, our sons and our brothers, listen to these words and let your conscience decide:

When the orders are immoral disobedience is a duty.

The Central Committee

Prairial 4, Year 79.

Appeal by the Central Committee of the National Guard to the soldiers of Versailles, 23 May 1871: *J.O.*, 24 May 1871.

3 The entry of the Versailles troops

The troops entered on the 22nd of May. Once fairly in, the work was comparatively easy; but they proceeded with great caution. It was said that [the Marquis de] Gallifet urged that he should take his cavalry, and scour the city. I believe that he could have done it on that day, for the Communists [a common description by outsiders for the Communards] were thoroughly demoralized; but it was thought to be too hazardous an operation for cavalry. The next morning the troops advanced unopposed as far as the Place de la Concorde. I have the word of an American friend, whose apartment looked upon the Place, that the strong barricade which connected the Rue St. Florentin with the Tuileries Gardens was then undefended, and that if the troops had advanced promptly they could have carried it without resistance; but while they sent forward their skirmishers, who found no one to skirmish with, and advanced with the utmost caution, a battery, followed by a battalion of the National Guard, galloped up from the Hôtel de Ville. The troops then began regular approaches. They entered the adjoining houses, passing from roof to roof, and occupying the upper windows, till finally they commanded the barricade, and fired down upon its defenders. They filled barrels with sand, and rolled them toward the barrier. Each barrel covered two skirmishers, who alternately rolled the barrel and picked off the defenders of the barricade if they ventured to show themselves. My informant saw a young and apparently good-looking woman spring upon the barricade, a red flag in her hand, and wave it defiantly at the troops. She was instantly shot dead. When the work was carried, an old woman was led out to be shot. She was placed with her back to the wall of the Tuileries Gardens, and, as the firing party leveled their pieces, she put her fingers to her nose, and worked them after the manner of the defiant in all ages, or, as Dickens expresses it, 'as if she were grinding an imaginary coffee-mill'.

Many of their strongest positions were abandoned by the insurgents, 163 having been turned by the troops. Those that resisted fell one after the other, carried in the way I have described. Indeed, I can see no possibility of a barricade holding out unless the adjacent houses are held too. That at the head of the Rue St. Florentin was of great strength, a regular work; for the Communists had several excellent engineers in their ranks, graduates of the military schools, men who had been disappointed under the Government in not meeting with the promotion they thought they deserved, and so joined the Commune. The ditch of the barricade St. Florentin was about sixteen feet deep. It made a convenient burying-ground. The dead Communists, men and women, were huddled into it, quicklime added, and the fosse filled up. As the pleasure-seeker enters the Rue de Rivoli from the Place de la Concorde he passes over the bodies of forty or fifty miserable wretches – most of them scoundrels of the deepest dye – but among them some wild fanatics, and some poor victims of the Commune, forced unwillingly into its ranks.

Much must be pardoned to soldiers heated with battle, and taught to believe every prisoner they take an incarnate devil. But making all allowances, there is no excuse for the wholesale butcheries committed by the troops. A friend of mine saw a house in the Boulevard Malesherbes visited by a squad of soldiers. They asked the *concierge* if there were any Communists concealed there. She answered that there were none. They searched the house, and found one. They took him out and shot him, and then shot her. One of the attachés of the [American] Legation saw in the Avenue d'Autin the bodies of six children, the eldest apparently not over fourteen, shot to death as *pétroleuses*,[1] suspected of carrying petroleum to fire the houses. There was no trial of any kind, no drum-head court-martial even, such as the laws of civilized warfare require under all circumstances. Any lieutenant ordered prisoners to be shot as the fancy took him, and no questions were asked. Many an innocent spectator perished in those days. An English officer had a narrow escape. He approached a crowd of prisoners halted for a moment on the Champs-Elysées; and when they moved on, the guard roped him in with the rest, and would not listen to a word of explanation. Happily he was able to attract the attention of the Marquis de Gallifet and explain his position. An officer[2] of high rank who was escorting a batch of prisoners to Versailles is said to have halted in the Bois [de Boulogne], ridden down the column, picked out those whose faces he particularly disliked, and had them shot on the spot. The number of lives taken after the defeat of the Commune can never be accurately known; but it was generally computed at the time to exceed the number of those lost in both sieges.

Petroleum next became the madness of the hour. Every woman carrying

---

[1] Incendiaries.

[2] In fact the Marquis de Gallifet.

Barricade at the junction of the rue de Rivoli and the rue Saint-Florentin (see description opposite). Intended to hinder Versailles troops entering Paris from the west, it was of little use in the street fighting, which occurred in the working-class districts further east.

a bottle was suspected of being a *pétroleuse*. The most absurd stories were told of its destructive properties. Organized bands of women were said to be patrolling the streets armed with bottles of petroleum. This they threw into the cellar windows, and then set fire to it. The windows were barred, and the cellars in Paris are universally built in stone and concrete. How they effected their purpose under these circumstances is not readily seen. If this was their *modus operandi*, they were the most inexpert incendiaries ever known. The Commune should blush for its pupils in crime. I do not believe in the petroleum story, and I do not think that one-third of the population believed in it. Yet such was the power of suspicion in those days, and such the distrust of one's neighbour, that every staid and sober house-keeper bricked up his cellar windows, and for weeks in the beautiful summer weather not an open window was to be seen on the lower stories. No doubt every second man thought it a great piece of folly thus to shut out light and air from his lower stories; but if he had not done as his neighbours did, he would have been denounced by them as a *pétroleux*.

An American observer's account of the entry of the
Versailles army; Hoffman, *Camp, Court and Siege*,
pp. 278–83.

64 Reflections on the street fighting

Reflections of a General Nature

One must realize that in civil war, as in an insurrection against a foreign invader, no quarter must be expected and consequently none must be given.

The insurrectionists must burn their boats from the start so that they are left with one choice only: victory or death.

Have no regard for public opinion or for persons or property; bear only one thought in mind: the ends justify the means. Our objectives are too lofty, the interests involved too important, the risks too great and the responsibility too serious; the heroes about to engage in this titanic struggle must not be swayed by any considerations that might hinder their success. All sentimentality is treason.

Street fighting does not take place in the street but in the houses; not in the open but under cover.

The general principles of street fighting are as follows:

The value of the individual fighter is more important than numerical superiority. One should accordingly restrict the field of action as much as possible; in other words, concentrate on man-to-man combat. A desperate man fighting for his own and his children's daily bread is worth ten soldiers fighting for their officer's pay.

The superiority of firearms must be neutralized by making their use impossible – in other words, by offering them no targets. If the enemy want to use their artillery they can only destroy what the rebels would have destroyed in any case. Who are they to use their guns on? No one is in sight. This is the crucial point.

A people's insurrection has no armaments; the enemy is well equipped. Hence the two sides of the situation: arrogant self-confidence on the part of the government, defeatism on the part of the governed. How can one fight bare-breasted against automatic rifles? This is how: render them useless by offering them no targets, and concentrate on destructive devices that damage material rather than persons. 'War on material!' should be our slogan in future wars. We must not hesitate to destroy what we cannot defend, even if it be an entire city. This is the reverse of bourgeois warfare where men, who cost nothing, are destroyed and property, which costs a great deal, is respected. If in 1870 we had had the courage to envisage a war of this nature France would not have been dismembered. Rostopchin saved his country by setting fire to Moscow. . . .[1]

The principle of destroying property rather than people is based on various arguments: first of all, the self-interest of the ruling classes, who are in love with property more than anything else. They will readily let down any form of government and even more readily betray their country

166   [1] When Napoleon I's troops occupied Moscow in September 1812.

if their property is at stake. They will also surrender without ceremony or conditions the moment their property is destroyed.

A logical and universally valid lesson may be drawn from this argument as far as class warfare is concerned. Any threat to property lowers its inflated value correspondingly. To ruin confidence in capital in all its forms should be the constant aim of class warfare. . . .

Final Preparations

. . . The street platoons will set up as many barricades as they can as fast as possible. They must bear in mind that the barricades are not intended for shelter, as the men defending them will be inside the houses, but to prevent enemy forces from circulating, to bring them to a halt and enable the insurrectionists posted in the houses to pelt them with explosives, furniture and anything else that can be used as a projectile.

It is therefore not necessary for the barricades to be perfectly constructed; they can very well be made of overturned carriages, doors taken off their hinges, furniture thrown out of windows, cobble-stones where these are available, beams, barrels etc.

In front of the barricades and as far as possible from them, the street should be strewn with broken bottles, planks with nails sticking out of them and, if there is a sufficient supply, a few bombs, which are to be concealed without being covered over. If few bombs are available they should be kept for throwing down from the tops of the houses. These measures are mainly for use against the cavalry. Not a single man is to remain behind the barricades.

During the Engagement

. . . As soon as contact has been made with the enemy, whether it be as they are approaching, in the actual target area or in the street, every means of destruction must be brought into play, especially incendiary materials. This is where buildings should be set on fire rather than occupied, and a few examples created to terrify the enemy. The dominant feature of present-day society is its cowardice, a logical consequence of self-interest and over-indulgence. These people must be faced with their own ruin and death and then they will submit to us unconditionally. This is true for international conflicts as it is for civil wars. . . .

The Last Stage

There is an alternative to this type of action which is part of the traditional war game but which sometimes succeeds: personal contact with the enemy.

The women, preceded by the children, rush towards the soldiers, grab their legs, embrace them, fraternize with them; then, while the soldiers stick their rifle-butts in the air the insurrectionists fire on their leaders.[1]

I went through this as an officer. There is not one of us who does not dread this critical moment, infinitely more dangerous than action. We know perfectly well that if contact is made it is the end. So we are given orders to avoid it at all costs. The only difficulty in establishing contact is knowing how to bypass the officers.

Besides this tactic one may also try raising fires at points distant from the scene of action, a tactical ruse that makes it easier for the squads in the streets and houses to operate. If we can deal with the enemy by making personal contact, all the better; if that fails it will still have facilitated action on the part of the local squads. . . .

Gustave-Paul Cluseret, the Commune's first Delegate of
War, reflects on the lessons to be learnt from the street
fighting at the end of the Commune: Cluseret, *Mémoires*,
vol. ii, pp. 273–89, abridged.

65 *The burnings justified*

We climbed to the lantern above the Town Hall of the 11th Arrondissement. Paris was burning! The Palais-Royal, the Ministry of Finance, the Rue de Rivoli, the Rue Royale formed a wall of fire before us. The leaping flames erected fantastic architectural shapes in the dark night – blazing arches, domes, ghostly buildings. To the right, the Porte Saint-Martin; to the left, the Hôtel de Ville, the Bastille and Bercy were belching forth blood-red columns of fire. Enormous white domes bursting skywards indicated powerful explosions. Every minute or so we saw flashes, within a stone's throw of us; it was the Père Lachaise blasting us with shell-fire.

As we stood there silent and still, watching the fire sweep across the city until the break of day, history seemed to unfold before our eyes: the Athenians leaving their city to be burned and sacked by the Persians rather than let themselves be captured; William the Silent choosing to let the Netherlands be swallowed up by the sea rather than allow the enemy to march over his kingdom; Saragossa defending itself inch by inch, burning its houses at the approach of the invader; Moscow in flames offering itself in sublime sacrifice to Russia!

If the Prussians had taken Paris by storm in January, and the Parisians had set the city on fire, the whole world would have applauded their heroism, and rightly so, for there is nothing more noble than passionate devotion to a great ideal. But now the same people who showed such heroism before the enemy are being called murderers, criminals, scum of the earth. Why? Because they are giving their lives for the Universal

[1] Compare Document 9, pp. 62–65, above.

Republic, because they have chosen, in defence of their religion, their conscience and their ideals, fired with wild enthusiasm, to let themselves be buried under the ruins of Paris rather than surrender to a coalition of tyrants a thousand times more brutal and immovable than the foreign invader.

What is patriotism if not the defence of our laws, our homes and our way of life against other gods, other laws, other ways of life that seek to impose themselves on us? For the people of Paris fighting for the Republic and for social reforms, Versailles, the feudal power, the exploiter of human misery, is just as much the enemy as the Prussians are, and as Napoleon I was for the Spaniards and the Russians. . . .

A Communard's justification of the burnings in Paris:
Lissagaray, *Les Huit Journées de mai*, pp. 102–4.

The return to order

FRENCH REPUBLIC

INHABITANTS OF PARIS

The French Army has come to your rescue.
Paris has been delivered.
At four o'clock our soldiers took the last rebel positions.
At last the fighting is over; order, work and security will reign once more.

Marshal MacMahon proclaims the return to order at the
end of the Commune, 28 May 1871: *M.P.*, vol. ii, p. 586.

Glossary of Names

ALLIX, Jules. 1818–97. Of bourgeois origin, law student, active in the June days of 1848 and in republican plots against Napoleon III. Exiled to Jersey, where he met Victor Hugo. For a time in Charenton asylum on his return to France. Very active during the siege in the field of education and women's employment and as Mayor of the 8th arrondissement during the Commune, of which he was a member. Condemned after the Commune, but sent to Charenton for five years. After the general amnesty of 1880 continued to propagate his schemes.

ARNOLD, Georges. 1837–1912. Architect, of no previous known political background. Became active in the National Guard during the siege. Elected to the Commune for the 18th arrondissement in the April by-elections; tried to represent the views of the National Guard Central Committee. Deported, and later employed as an architect by the City of Paris.

ARNOULD, Arthur. 1833–95. Son of a professor at the Sorbonne and one of the editors of the main republican opposition paper, *La Marseillaise*, in the late 1860s. Member of the Commune for the 4th arrondissement, and one of the leaders of the 'minority'. Escaped to Switzerland, where he wrote a useful history of the Commune.

AVRIAL, Augustin. 1840–1904. Engineering worker, active in the International at the end of the Empire. During the siege took part in the uprising of 31 October, and in the fighting at the beginning and the end of the Commune.

Member for the 11th arrondissement. Escaped to London, and for a time worked with other ex-Communards in Alsace, which Germany had won in the war. After the amnesty worked on French railways, invented a sewing-machine that bore his name, and supported Allemanist socialists (Allemane was also an ex-Communard).

BABICK, Jules. 1820–1902. Perfumer and member of the International. Signed *l'Affiche rouge* issued by the Vigilance Committee in January 1871. Member of the Commune for the 10th arrondissement, and noted for his military bearing – he wore a red sash over his National Guard uniform – and for his prophetic appearance. Belonged to a religious group called the fusionists. Escaped to Switzerland.

BARRON, Louis. 1847–1914. Son of an ex-soldier, he too served in the army for a time. Fought in 1870, but was discharged for health reasons. Came to Paris after the proclamation of the Commune and joined Rossel's staff with the help of a recommendation from Courbet. Escaped from Paris and worked with private companies until recognized in 1876 and deported. Wrote a valuable account of his experiences during the Commune.

BILLIORAY, Alfred. 1841–76. House-painter. Member of the National Guard Central Committee and of the Commune for the 14th arrondissement. Elected to the second Committee of Public Safety. Died in deportation.

BLANQUI, Auguste. 1805–81. Professional revolutionary. Imprisoned for belonging to the secret societies of the 1820s and 1830s. Freed after the 1848 revolution, he was active against the new government and led the invasion of the Chambre de Députés in May 1848. Imprisoned again several times, he was nicknamed 'l'enfermé'. His political ideas were based on the doctrines of Babeuf and his 'conspiracy of equals' of 1796; the Blanquists were the leading conspirators at the end of the Empire. During the siege Blanqui bitterly attacked the Government of National Defence in his paper *La Patrie en Danger*. Condemned for his part in the 31 October uprising, of which he had been made one of the leaders, and arrested on the eve of the Commune. Thiers refused to exchange him against the Archbishop of Paris and other hostages who were shot during the last week. Imprisoned and freed in 1879.

CHALAIN, Louis. 1845–1902. Jeweller. Member of the Commune for the 17th arrondissement. Deported. Later joined Allemanists (see Avrial).

CHARDON, J.-B. 1839–1900. Tin worker. Blanquist member of the Commune for the 13th arrondissement. Member of the War Commission and military commander of the police. Escaped arrest.

CLÉMENT, J.-B. 1836–1903. Singer and popular poet. Arrested several times under the Second Empire. Member of the Commune for the 18th arrondissement and of the Education Commission. Escaped to London. Active in the socialist movement in France in the 1880s.

CLUSERET, General Gustave-Paul. 1823–1900. Ex-regular army officer who had also fought in the American Civil War and acted as a professional revolutionary in South America and Ireland. Was appointed the Commune's first Delegate of War; arrested at the beginning of May, and then acquitted of charges of incompetence. Escaped to London, where he wrote his *Mémoires*, the last

chapters being concerned with the street battles of the end of the Commune.

COURBET, Gustave. 1819–77. Painter. President of the Artists' Federation. Elected to the Commune for the 6th arrondissement in the April by-elections. Made financially liable for the reconstruction of the Vendôme Column, he was forced to flee to Switzerland.

DELESCLUZE, Charles. 1809–71. Jacobin and republican journalist, active during 1848 revolution and exiled in 1849. Arrested on his return to France for plotting against Napoleon III and imprisoned on Devil's Island. Edited one of the leading republican opposition papers, *Le Réveil*, after 1868. Elected to the National Assembly in February 1871, he then resigned to become a member of the Commune for the 11th arrondissement. Member of the Committee of Public Safety and appointed the Commune's last Delegate of War. Died on a barricade.

DMITRIEFF, Élisabeth. 1851–1910. Daughter of a Russian nobleman, she married a Russian colonel in order to escape from Russia and study in Switzerland. In London she met Marx and was a member of the International. During the Commune she organized the Women's Union for the Defence of Paris as a branch of the International. Escaped and returned to Russia; married a political prisoner condemned to Siberia, where she died.

FERRÉ, Théophile. 1840–71. Blanquist, and member of the Vigilance Committee in the 18th arrondissement. Member of the Commune for the same district. Next in command to Rigault at the Prefecture of Police. Executed.

FRANKEL, Léo. 1844–95. Son of a Hungarian doctor. Active in the International in Lyon and later as a jeweller in Paris. Met Marx in London when first exiled from Hungary. Member of the central council of the International and then of the Commune for the 13th 171 arrondissement. Presided over the Commission for Labour and Exchange. Escaped to London. Was later active in the socialist movement both in Hungary, until arrested, and then in Paris again, where he died and was buried in a red flag in the Père-Lachaise cemetery.

GÉRARDIN, Charles. 1843–1912. Commercial traveller. Member of the Central Committee of the Twenty Arrondissements and of the Commune, for the 17th arrondissement. Friend of Rossel. Exile in London.

GROUSSET, Paschal. 1845–1909. Republican journalist in late 1860s. Member of the Commune for the 18th arrondissement and Delegate for Foreign Affairs. Jacobin. Escaped from deportation and later became a socialist Deputy.

JOURDE, Francis. 1843–93. Bank clerk. Member of the National Guard Central Committee, and then of the Commune for the 5th arrondissement. Delegate to the Ministry of Finance. Deported.

LANGEVIN, Pierre. 1843–1913. Founder member of the Engineering Workers' Trades Union in 1868 and, in the following year, of the Federation of Parisian Workers' Organizations. Member of the International and active in the National Guard during the siege. Unsuccessful Revolutionary Socialist candidate in the national elections of February 1871. Elected to the Commune for the 15th arrondissement. Escaped from Paris and worked for a time in an engineering factory in Alsace until expelled from there to London in 1876. After the general amnesty of 1880 returned to Bordeaux and worked on the railways. At the end of the century moved back to Paris where he was active in the co-operative movement.

LEMEL, Nathalie. 1827–1921. Worked as a bookbinder; separated from her husband. Joined the International and founded a workers' restaurant with Varlin, which functioned during the siege. Active in the clubs; helped

Élisabeth Dmitrieff form the Women's Union. Deported.

LONGUET, Charles. 1839–1903. Law student and republican journalist in the 1860s. Translated the statutes of the International into French. Exiled to London, returned to Paris in September 1870. Member of the Central Committee of the Twenty Arrondissements. Unsuccessful Revolutionary Socialist candidate in the February elections. Member of the National Guard Central Committee, which appointed him editor of the *Journal Officiel* after 18 March. Elected to the Commune for the 16th arrondissement in the April by-elections. Escaped to London, and married Marx's eldest daughter, Jenny. On his return to Paris worked on Clemenceau's paper, *La Justice*.

MACMAHON, Marshal. 1808–93. Created Marshal of France in 1859. Commanded French army that surrendered at Sedan. Led Versailles troops against the Commune. Became President of the Republic on Thiers's resignation in 1873 and himself resigned in 1879 because of republican opposition.

MALON, Benoît. 1841–93. Member of the International, and active during the siege as Deputy Mayor of the 17th arrondissement; elected to the National Assembly in February 1871, but then resigned to become member of the Commune for the 17th arrondissement. Escaped to Switzerland, where he wrote a history of the Commune. In the 1880s joined the Workers' Party (*Parti ouvrier*) until he broke away to become an Independent Socialist.

MIOT, Jules. 1810–83. Chemist. Deported for republican views after Napoleon III's *coup d'état* in 1851. Blanquist and member of the International in the 1860s. Deputy Mayor of the 8th arrondissement during the siege, then member of the Commune for the 19th. Escaped to Switzerland.

MOREAU, Édouard. 1836–71. Writer and businessman; not involved in politics before 1870. Active in the National Guard during the siege and on its Central Committee after 18 March. Shot during the last week.

PYAT, Félix. 1810–89. Law student, journalist and successful writer of melodramas in the 1830s. Member of the 'Mountain' in the 1849 Assembly, until forced to flee to Switzerland after the June 1849 revolt. Returned in 1869, and edited a leading republican opposition paper. In February 1871 founded a second paper, Le Vengeur, after the suppression of his first, and elected to the National Assembly. Resigned at the beginning of March. Member of the Commune for the 10th arrondissement, and of the Committee of Public Safety. Escaped to England. Republican Deputy in the 1880s.

RASTOUL, Paul. 1835–75. Doctor from a wealthy family; no previously known political activity until he joined the National Guard during the siege. Member of the Commune for the 10th arrondissement. Condemned to deportation and drowned while trying to escape from L'Île des Pins.

RÉGÈRE, Dominique. 1816–93. Veterinary surgeon who had had to flee after the 1851 coup d'état. Member of the Commune for the 5th arrondissement. Deported.

RIGAULT, Raoul. 1846–71. Son of a leading wealthy republican. Member of the Commune for the 8th arrondissement. In charge of the Prefecture of Police. Shot during the last week.

ROSSEL, Louis. 1844–71. Army officer who joined Paris after 18 March out of patriotic disgust with the National Assembly for making peace with Germany. Delegate of War after Cluseret's arrest, until he resigned. Escaped arrest by the Commune, but was caught after its fall and executed.

SERRAILLIER, Auguste. 1840–? Shoemaker who joined the International in London; friend of Marx. Sent by the General Council of the International to Paris in September 1870, and again in March 1871. Elected to the Commune in the April by-elections for the 2nd arrondissement. Member of the Commission of Labour and Exchange. Escaped to London.

THEISZ, Albert. 1839–81. Bronzeworker. Member of the International and of the Commune for the 18th arrondissement. In charge of the Commune's postal service. Escaped to London.

THIERS, Adolphe. 1797–1877. Lawyer and historian who belonged to the liberal opposition under Charles X and played an important role in getting the crown offered to Louis-Philippe in July 1830. Premier and Minister of Foreign Affairs in 1836 and 1840. Responsible for plan to fortify Paris in 1840s. Defended conservative cause after 1848, but opposed Napoleon's coup d'état. Deputy again in 1863 and elder statesman of the opposition and leading Orléanist. Acted as negotiator between the government in Paris and Bismarck during the siege. Made 'Chief Executive of the Republic' in February 1871 and thus in charge of the defeat of the Commune. Resigned in 1873.

TRIDON, Gustave. 1841–71. Son of a wealthy landowner. Journalist and historian of the Hébertistes of the first Revolution. Blanqui's second-in-command. Elected Deputy in the national elections of February 1871. Resigned in protest against the peace treaty. Member of the Commune for the 5th arrondissement, but already very ill. Escaped to Brussels, where he died.

URBAIN, Raoul. 1837–1902. Schoolteacher, and the son of one. In the 1860s formed a democratic primary school, which had no religious education, and 173 was accordingly soon forced to close by the local Mayor. Signed *L'Affiche rouge* of January 1871. Elected to the Commune for the 7th arrondissement and remained active within that arrondissement, ensuring that the red flag was flown on all public buildings and encouraging the establishment of non-religious schools. Deported. In 1890s active in the co-operative movement.

VAILLANT, Édouard. 1840–1915. Engineer and science student. Studied in Germany until outbreak of war in 1870. Blanquist and member of the International. Member of the Central Committee of the National Guard, and of the Commune for the 8th arrondissement. Delegate of Education. In exile met Marx in London, but on return to France after 1880 became leading organizer of the Blanquist Party. Deputy for Paris from 1893 and leading figure next to Jaurès in the United Socialist Party *(Parti socialiste unifié)* formed in 1905.

VALLÈS, Jules. 1832–85. Son of a provincial schoolteacher, journalist and novelist in the revolutionary Left Bank *bohème* in the 1860s. Active in the National Guard during the siege and arrested for his part in the 31 October uprising. Founded *Le Cri du Peuple* in February 1871. Member of the Commune for the 15th arrondissement. Escaped to London.

VARLIN, Eugène. 1839–71. Bookbinder, son of peasant farmer. Active in the strike movement of 1860s, and militant member of the International. Member of the Central Committee of the National Guard and of the Commune for the 6th arrondissement. Killed during the last week.

VERMOREL, Auguste. 1841–71. Journalist and writer. Edited the leading socialist paper of the 1860s. Imprisoned after the uprising of 31 October. Member of the Commune for the 18th arrondissement. Wounded on the barricades and died in prison shortly afterwards.

VÉSINIER, Pierre. 1826–1902. Journalist and man of letters. Exiled after Napoleon III's *coup d'état* in 1851; for a time a clockmaker in Switzerland, where he helped Eugène Sue publish his novel of low life in Paris, *Les Mystères de Paris*. Expelled from Switzerland, he joined the International in London, where he was active among the French exiles, but in opposition to Marx and the General Council. Member of the Vigilance Committee of the 20th arrondissement during the siege. Elected to the Commune in the April by-elections for the 1st arrondissement. Worked on several papers, and was put in charge of the Commune's *Journal Officiel* in May. Escaped to London.

Bibliography

Books on the Commune
The best English accounts are S. Edwards, *The Paris Commune: 1871*, London, 1971, New York, 1973, which is the most detailed and covers recent research and archival material, and the stimulating classic by F. Jellinek, *The Paris Commune of 1871*, first published in 1937 and reissued in New York in 1965 and in London in 1971. The best contemporary account, that by the Communard Prosper Lissagaray, has often been reprinted in French; Marx's daughter Eleanor translated it into English in 1886, reprinted in New York, 1969. Edith Thomas's important study of women during the Commune was translated as *The Women Incendiaries*, New York 1966, London 1967. For a general coverage of the politics of the end of the Empire and the beginning of the Third Republic there is R. L. Williams, *The*

French Revolution of 1870–1871, London, 1969. The military history of the war against the Prussians is chronicled by Michael Howard, *The Franco-Prussian War*, London, 1961. A general though condescending account of the war and the Commune is that by A. Horne, *The Fall of Paris*, London, 1965. E. Mason, *The Paris Commune*, is a conservative though useful account written in 1930, reissued in 1967 in New York.

A useful companion volume to the present selection is a selection of documents from the Commune dealing particularly with social issues, accompanied by passages taken from the writings of later anarchists, socialists and Marxists commenting on the Commune, by E. Schulkind, *The Paris Commune of 1871: The View from the Left*, London, 1972. This also has a short bibliography of books in French, and fuller bibliographies can be found in Edwards, Jellinek and Williams above. J. Rougerie has published two very important selections of documents in French, which are essential for all studies of the Commune: *Procès des Communards*, Paris, 1964, and *Paris libre: 1871*, Paris, 1971.

Sources used for the documents:

A.H.G. Archives Historiques de la Guerre, Vincennes.

Bulletin communal, 'Organe des Clubs', Paris.

E.P. Enquête parlementaire sur l'insurrection du 18 mars, 3 vols., Versailles, 1872.

J.O. Journal Officiel de la République Française, Paris.

Le Combat, Paris.

Le Cri du Peuple, Paris.

Le Mercure de France, Paris.

Le Père Duchêne, Paris.

Le Prolétaire, Paris.

Lettres au Père Duchêne pendant la Commune de Paris, Marx-Engels-Lenin Institute (Moscow), Paris, 1934.

Le Vengeur, Paris.

M.P. Les Murailles politiques françaises, 2 vols., Paris, 1871.

P.V.C. G. Bourgin and G. Henriot (edd.), *Procès-Verbaux de la Commune de 1871*, 2 vols., 1924, 1945.

The Times, London.

A. ADAMOV, *Anthologie de la Commune*, Paris, 1959.

H. D'ALMÉRAS, *La Vie parisienne pendant le siège et sous la Commune*, Paris, s.d. (1925).

L. BARRON, *Sous le drapeau rouge*, Paris, 1889.

G. BOURGIN, *La Guerre de 1870–1871 et la Commune*, Paris, 1939.

G.-P. CLUSERET, *Mémoires*, 3 vols., Paris, 1887.

V. D'ESBŒUFS, *La Vérité sur la Commune par un ancien proscrit*, Paris, 1879–80.

P. FONTOULIEU, *Les Églises de Paris sous la Commune*, Paris, 1873.

W. HOFFMAN, *Camp, Court and Siege*, New York, 1877.

J. LEIGHTON, *Paris under the Commune*, London, 1871.

P.-O. LISSAGARAY, *Les Huit Journées de mai*, Brussels, 1871, Paris, 1968.

J. ROCHER (ed.), *Lettres de communards et de militants de la Première International à Marx, Engels et autres dans les journées de la Commune de Paris en 1871*, Paris, 1934.

L.-N. ROSSEL, *Mémoires, procès et correspondance*, Paris, 1960.

J. ROUGERIE, *Procès des communards*, Paris, 1964.

M. VUILLAUME, *Mes Cahiers rouges au temps de la Commune*, Cahiers de la Quinzaine (IXe série), Paris, 1908–14.
175

Chronology

1870	*19 July*	France declares war on Prussia.
	4 September	News of French defeat at Sedan by the Prussian army and capture of the Emperor Napoleon III. Empire overthrown in Paris and Republic proclaimed. Formation of the Government of National Defence in Paris.
	15 September	First proclamation by the newly formed Central Committee of the Twenty Arrondissements.
	18 September	Prussians begin to besiege Paris.
	5 October	Central Committee of the Twenty Arrondissements appeals for elections.
	8 October	Failure of demonstrations led by the Central Committee of the Twenty Arrondissements.
	31 October	News of surrender of French army at Metz leads to unsuccessful uprising in Paris.
	4 November	Mayoral elections held in Paris following arrest of those involved in events of 31 October.
1871	*5 January*	Prussians begin to bombard Paris.
	6 January	Central Committee of the Twenty Arrondissements issues *L'Affiche rouge*.
	28 January	Armistice between France and Prussia announced.
	8 February	Elections held throughout France for a National Assembly.
	12 February	First session of the National Assembly at Bordeaux.
	20 and 23 February	Foundation of a 'Revolutionary Socialist party'. Thiers forms a ministry.
	24 February	Paris National Guard meets to form its own federation and Central Committee. Demonstration at the Place de la Bastille.
	26 and 27 February	Crowds seize the cannon at Place de Wagram and transport them to the eastern suburbs.
	1 March	Ceremonial entry of the Prussians into Paris. Peace treaty passed by the National Assembly.
176	*15 March*	National Guard elects its Central Committee.

16 March	Thiers arrives in Paris.
18 March	Government attempt to seize cannon on Montmartre and elsewhere fails. Thiers and his government flee Paris for Versailles. National Guard Central Committee takes over the Hôtel de Ville.
19 March	Central Committee of the National Guard announces elections in Paris for a Commune.
22 March	Commune proclaimed at Lyon.
23 March	Commune proclaimed at Marseille.
25 March	Collapse of Commune at Lyon.
26 March	Elections in Paris for the Commune.
28 March	Proclamation of the Paris Commune.
29 March	First decrees issued by the Commune.
30 March	Outbreak of civil war between Paris and National Government at Versailles.
4 April	Retreat of the Communard forces. First prisoners taken. Cluseret made Commune's first Delegate of War. Defeat of the Commune at Marseille.
6 April	Public burning of the guillotine in the 11th arrondissement.
11 April	Foundation of the Women's Union for the Defence of Paris and for Aid to the Wounded.
14 April	First meeting of the Artists' Federation under Courbet's presidency.
16 April	By-elections to the Commune. Decree on abandoned workshops.
19 April	Commune's 'Declaration to the French People'.
28 April	Proposal to form a Committee of Public Safety. Decree forbidding bakers' night-work. Commission for the Organization of Education created.
1 May	Creation of the first Committee of Public Safety. Cluseret dismissed and arrested; Rossel replaces him at the Ministry of War. Versailles troops begin to bombard the capital.
6 May	Decree establishing the first technical school of the Commune.
9 May	Fall of the fort at Issy; Rossel resigns. New members appointed to the Committee of Public Safety.
10 May	Delescluze appointed civilian Delegate of War. Peace treaty between France and Germany signed at Frankfurt.

	15 May	Minority declaration against the Committee of Public Safety.
	16 May	Demolition of the Vendôme Column.
	21 May	Last full session of the Commune; Cluseret freed. Versailles troops enter Paris.
	25 May	Last session of the Commune held in the mairie of the 12th arrondissement. Death of Delescluze on a barricade.
	27 May	Capture of the Buttes de Chaumont. Execution of fallen Communards in the Père-Lachaise cemetery.
	28 May	Last barricades fall. Death of Varlin.
	November	First executions of condemned Communards.
1872	May	First deportations of prisoners. International declared illegal in France.
1880		General amnesty.

Acknowledgments

Bibliothèque Historique de la Ville de Paris frontispiece, pp. 51, 57, 97; Bulloz p. 8; Victoria and Albert Museum pp. 11 (*top*), 19, 25, 29 (*top right*), 29 (*bottom row*), 75, 85, 121 (*top*), 149; Bibliothèque Nationale pp. 11 (*bottom*), 77; Claus Henning (map) pp. 12–13; Archives livre Club Diderot, photothèque Laffont p. 29 (*top left*); Roger-Viollet p. 29 (*top centre*); *Le Monde Illustré* pp. 43 (*bottom*), 159 (*bottom*); Giraudon pp. 67, 111; Archives Nationales p. 99; *L'Illustration* p. 129; Collection Duchemin-Kothelova, photothèque Laffont p. 135; *Illustrated London News* 145; *Charivari* p. 151; Mancell Collection pp. 159 (*top*), 165.

Index

179

Marseille 9, 30, 41
Marx, Karl 158, 171–4; and anarchism 10; on Commune 30, 34, 37, 66; and Frankel 27; and International 15; on revolution 33
Miot, Jules 91n., 94, 103n., 172; and Committee of Public Safety 32, 86–8; and Vendôme Column 147
Molière, Jean-Baptiste 151
Montmartre 14, 24–5, 56–8, 62–5; Sacré-Cœur Church 40
Moreau, Édouard 32, 76, 79, 173

NAPOLEON III 9, 14, 48, 50, 74, 104, 112, 147n., 170; *coup d'état* by 16, 21–2, 103, 162, 173–4
National Guard: and Civil War 32–3, 94, 98, 102; during Commune 36, 39, 45, 51, 74, 127, 131–3; during Franco-Prussian War 75n., 126; during last week 162–3; on 18 March 58–65; history of 21–6; hostility to National Government 48, 50–2
National Guard Central Committee: and Civil War 33, 76, 84–5; during Commune 32, 66, 78–81, 134; during last week 163; formation of 22, 50–2; on 18 March 26, 103n.; and elections 47; members of 170, 173
Newton, Isaac 153

PARIS: Archbishop of 30; industry and social structure 14–15, 28–9; Place de la Bourse 102; revolutionary tradition of 9, 16; rue de Rivoli 164, 165, 168; siege of 23–6, 47, 52; *see also* Belleville, Hôtel de Ville, Montmartre, Père-Lachaise cemetery, Tuileries Palace, Vendôme Column
Père-Lachaise cemetery 10, 171
Picard, Ernest 54, 117
Prefecture of Police 19, 40, 159, 173
Proudhon, Pierre-Joseph 30, 37–8, 76, 93n., 122
Pyat, Félix 29, 30, 34, 91, 152, 154, 173

RASTOUL, Dr Paul 87, 173
Régère, Dominique-Théodore 77, 87, 91, 173
Renan, Ernest 101
Revolution (1789) 15, 21, 68, 82, 93, 109, 142, 158; *see also* Jacobinism
Revolution (1793) 9, 16, 33, 42, 74, 90, 91, 93, 110, 112, 122, 139, 150, 161
Revolution (1830) 9, 15, 51
Revolution (1848) 15–16, 21, 28, 112, 170–3; history of 9, 26, 39–40, 122, 140, 158;

referred to by Communards 51, 90, 97, 125, 143, 145, 162
Revolution (4 September 1870) 8, 17, 69, 90
Revolution (18 March 1871) 11, 25–6, 56–7, 81, 83, 95–6, 124, 158, 161–2
Rigault, Raoul 27–8, 29, 30, 91, 173
Robespierre, Maximilien *see* Jacobinism
Rossel, Louis-Nathaniel 31–4, 78, 84–5, 103n., 158, 162, 173
Rousseau, Jean-Jacques 117

SACRÉ-COEUR Church 40
Seraillier, Auguste 92, 133, 173
Socialism; class feeling 96; in clubs 102–6; in Commune 39, 67–9, 71–2, 80, 112, 122–39, 152
Social legislation 34–6, 112–33

THEISZ, Albert 66, 92, 137, 139, 173
Thiers, Adolphe 11, 27, 103n., 116, 135, 143, 172, 173; and Blanqui 30; and Civil War 38, 158; and Freemasons 40; heads National Government 23–6; and social nature of Commune 38
Tridon, Gustave 28, 90, 92, 173
Tuileries Palace 40, 145, 159, 168

VAILLANT, Édouard 29, 174; on Committee of Public Safety 33, 87, 88, 90, 92; heads Education Commission 35–7, 112, 114–15; on theatres 150–2, 154–5
Vallès, Jules 75, 174; on Committee of Public Safety 89, 92; and Declaration to French People 78; as journalist 28; on proclamation of Commune 66, 75, 140
Varlin, Eugène 107, 137, 172, 174
Vendôme Column 40–1, 104, 141, 146–8, 149, 171
Vermorel, Auguste 88–9, 92, 138, 174
Vésinier, Pierre 90, 100, 153–5, 174
Villiers de l'Isle Adam, P. H. 40, 140, 142
Vinoy, General 56, 117
Voltaire 154

WOMEN, role of: on barricades 163, 167; and clothing manufacture 36, 131–3, 135–6; and education 37, 112, 114–17; and 18 March 103n.; *see also under* Clubs
Women's Union for the Defence of Paris and for Aid to the Wounded 36, 134, 136, 171